RELAXING MANDALA COLORING BOOK FOR BEGINNERS

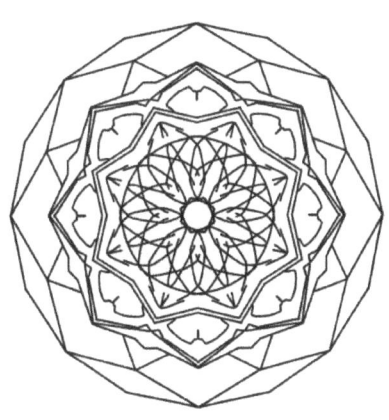

Easy Mandalas for Kids and Adults

65 Mandalas To Be Colored

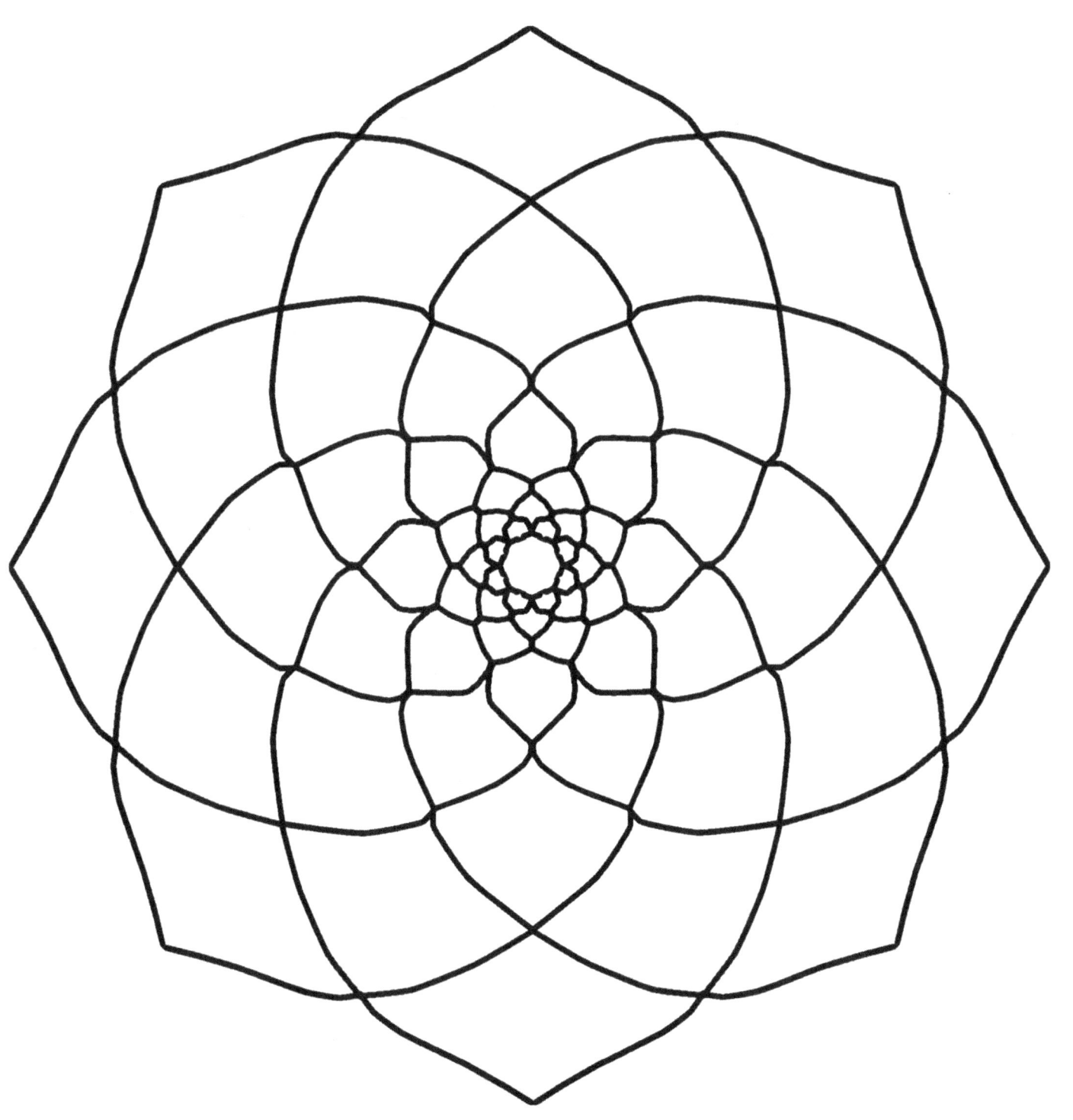

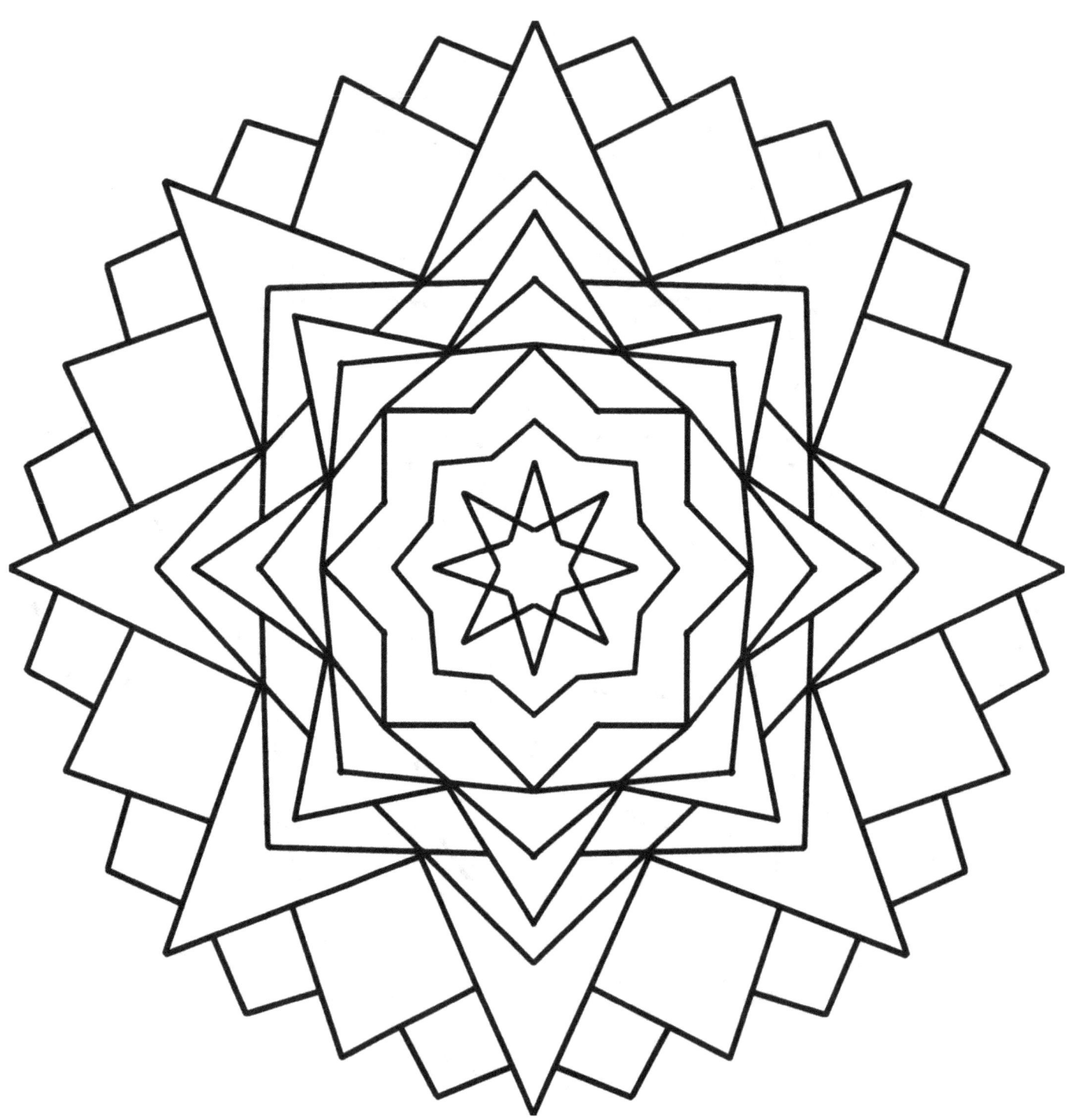

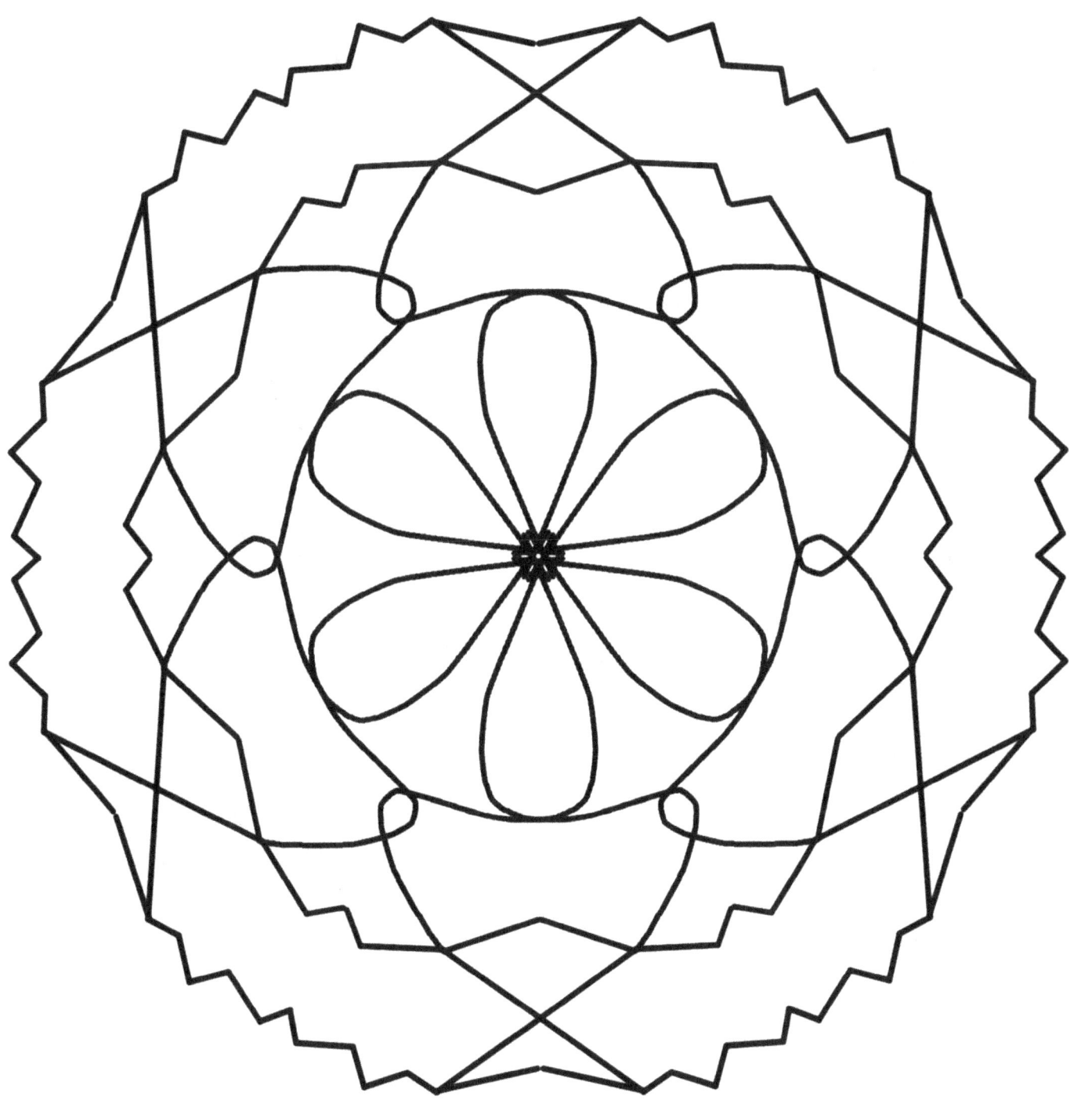

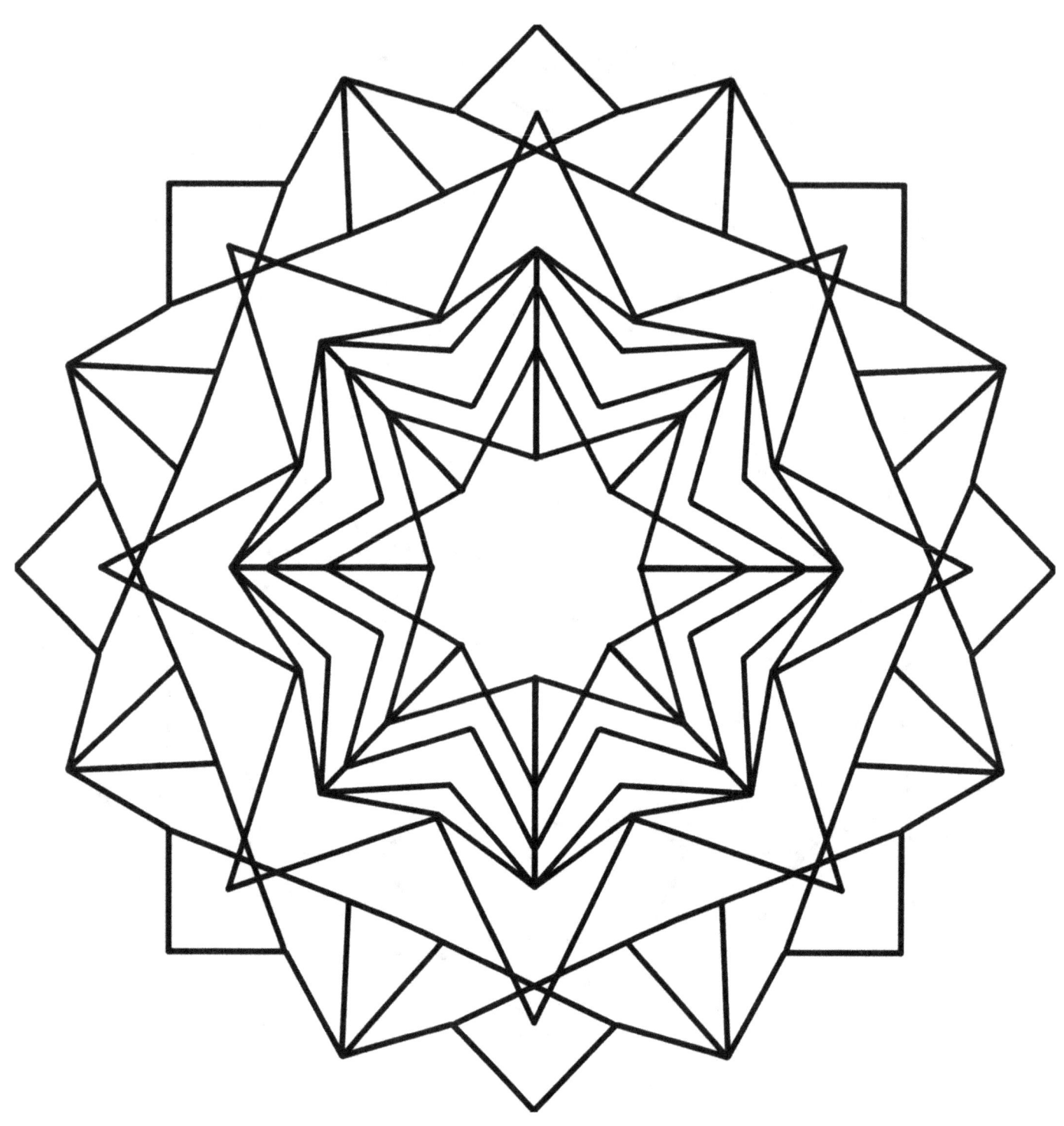

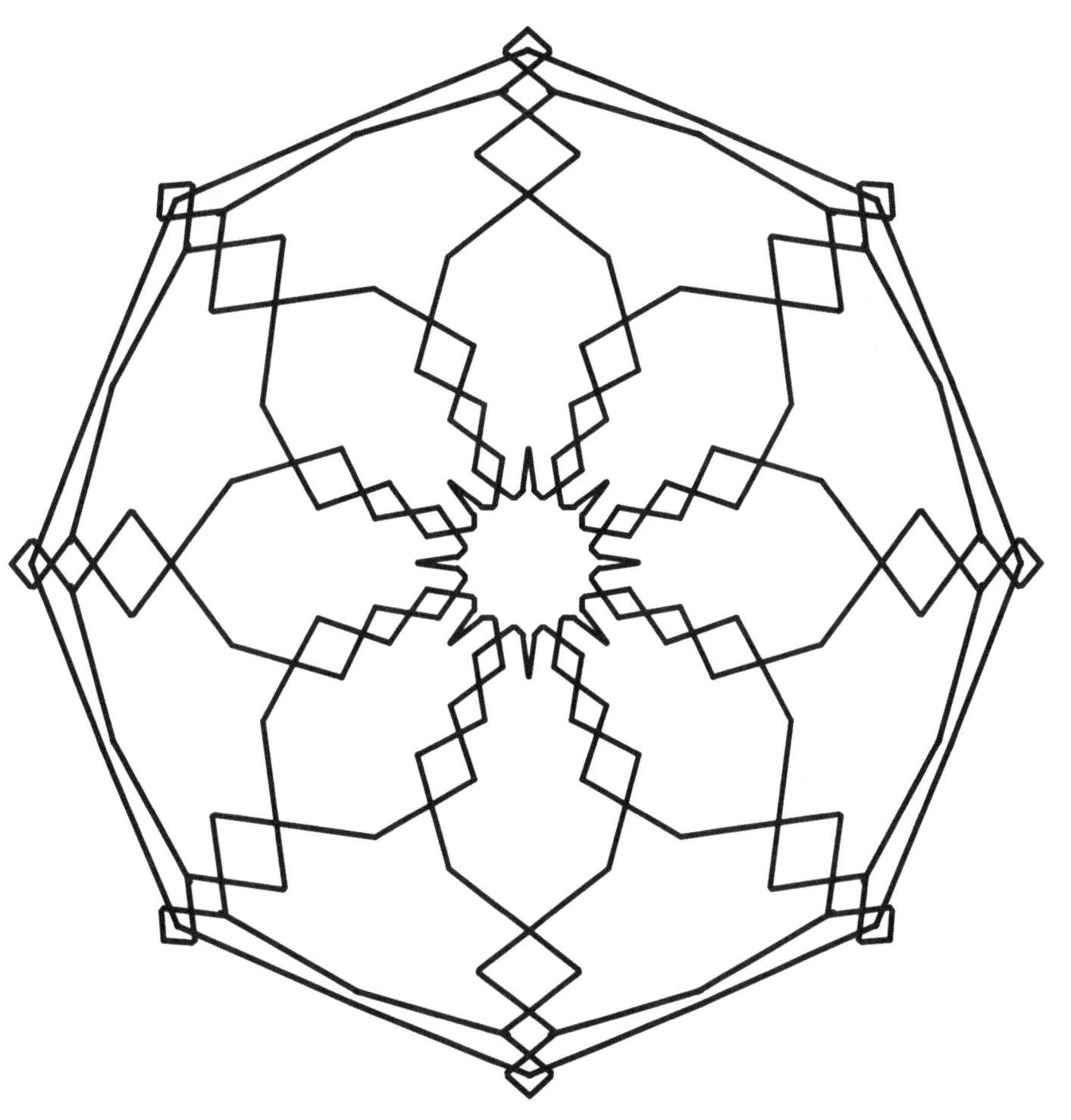

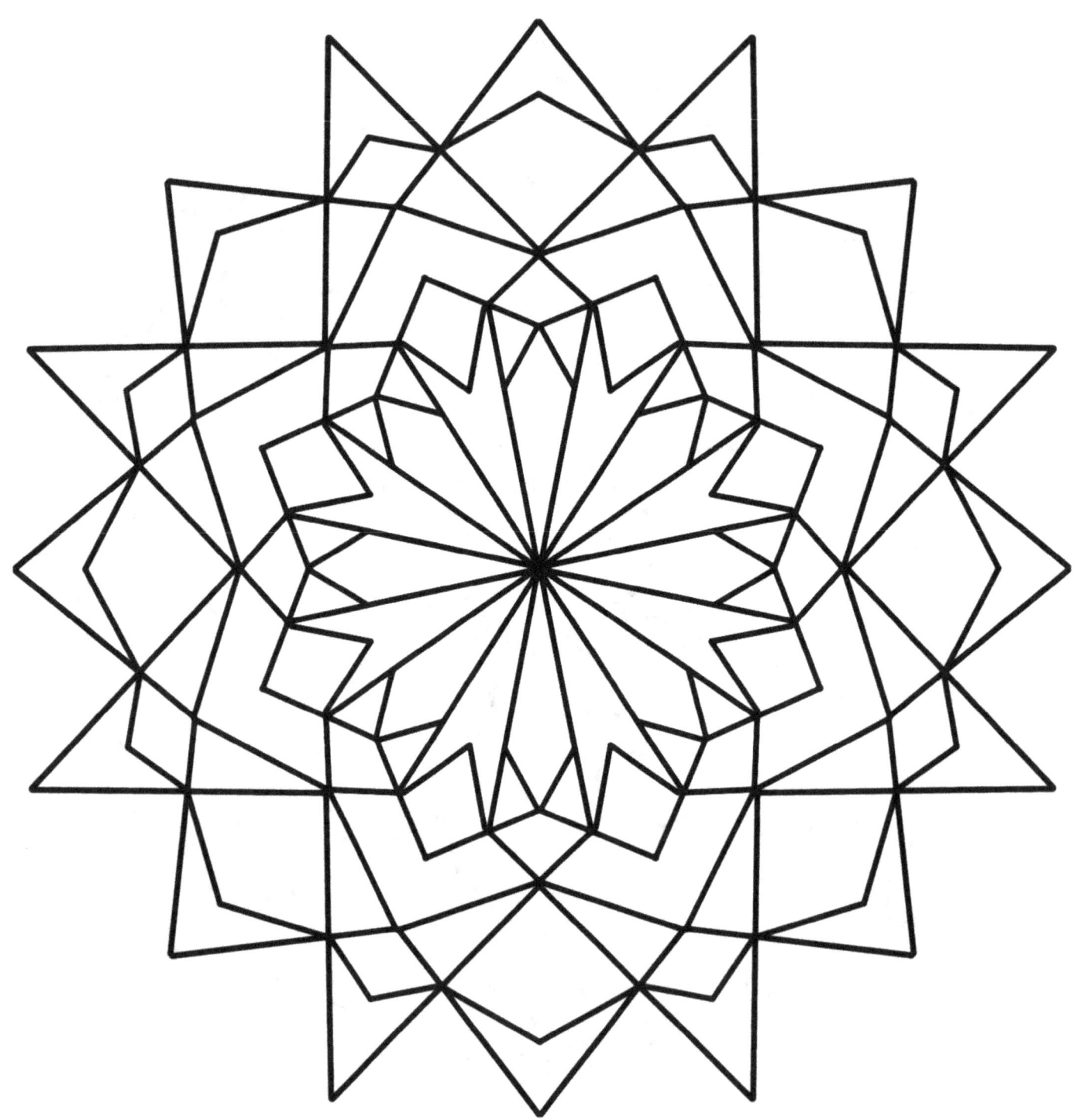

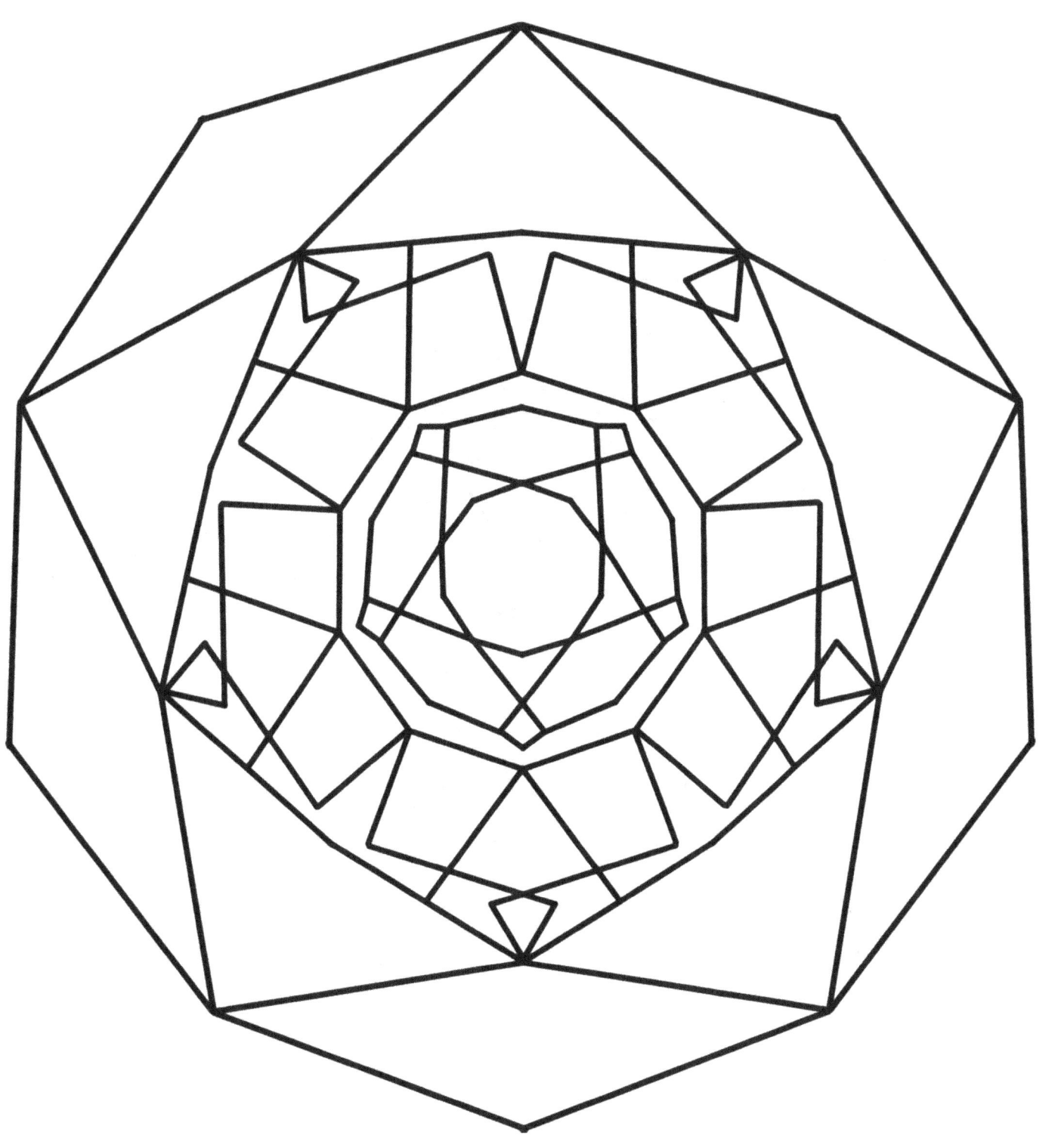

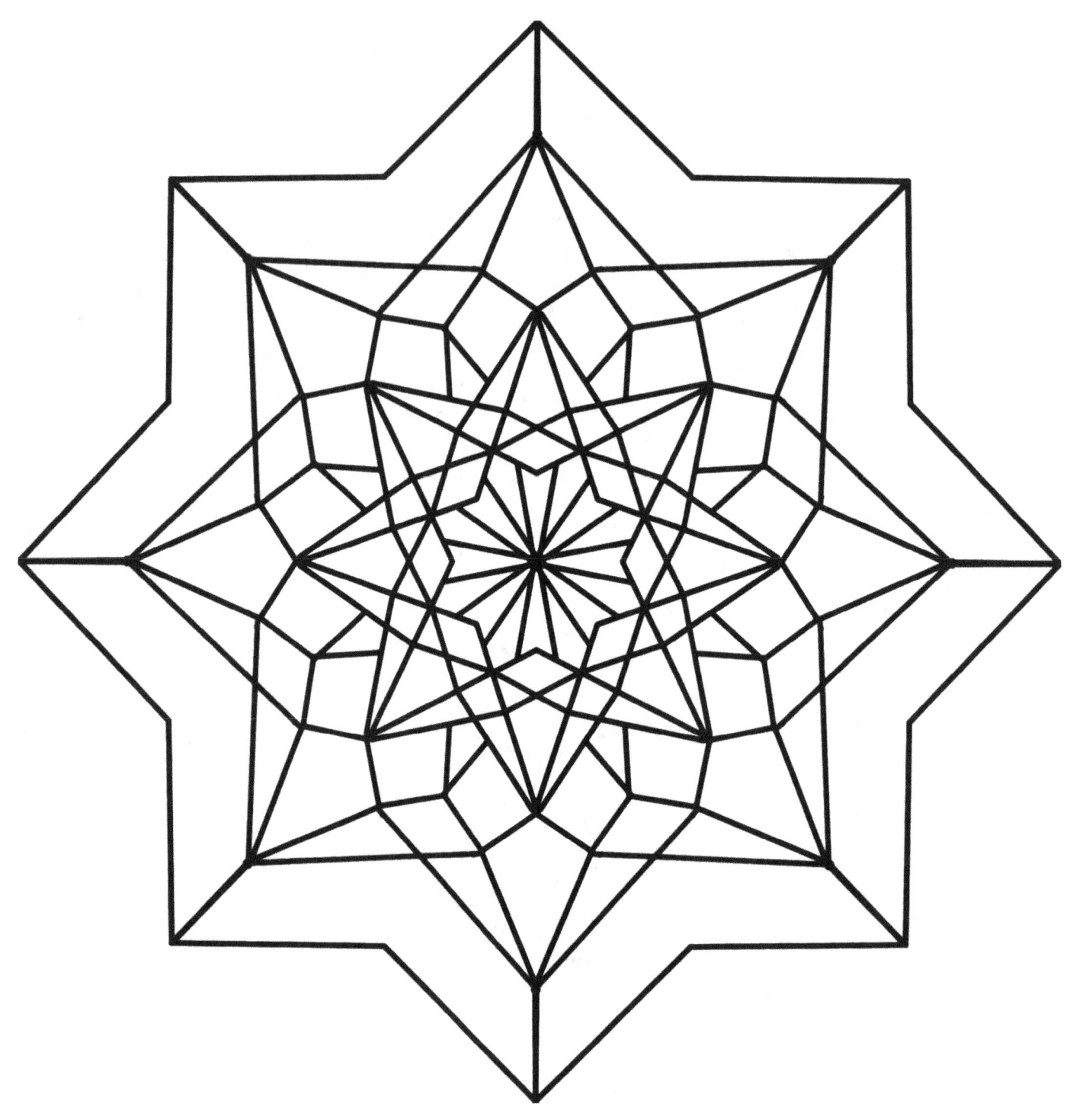

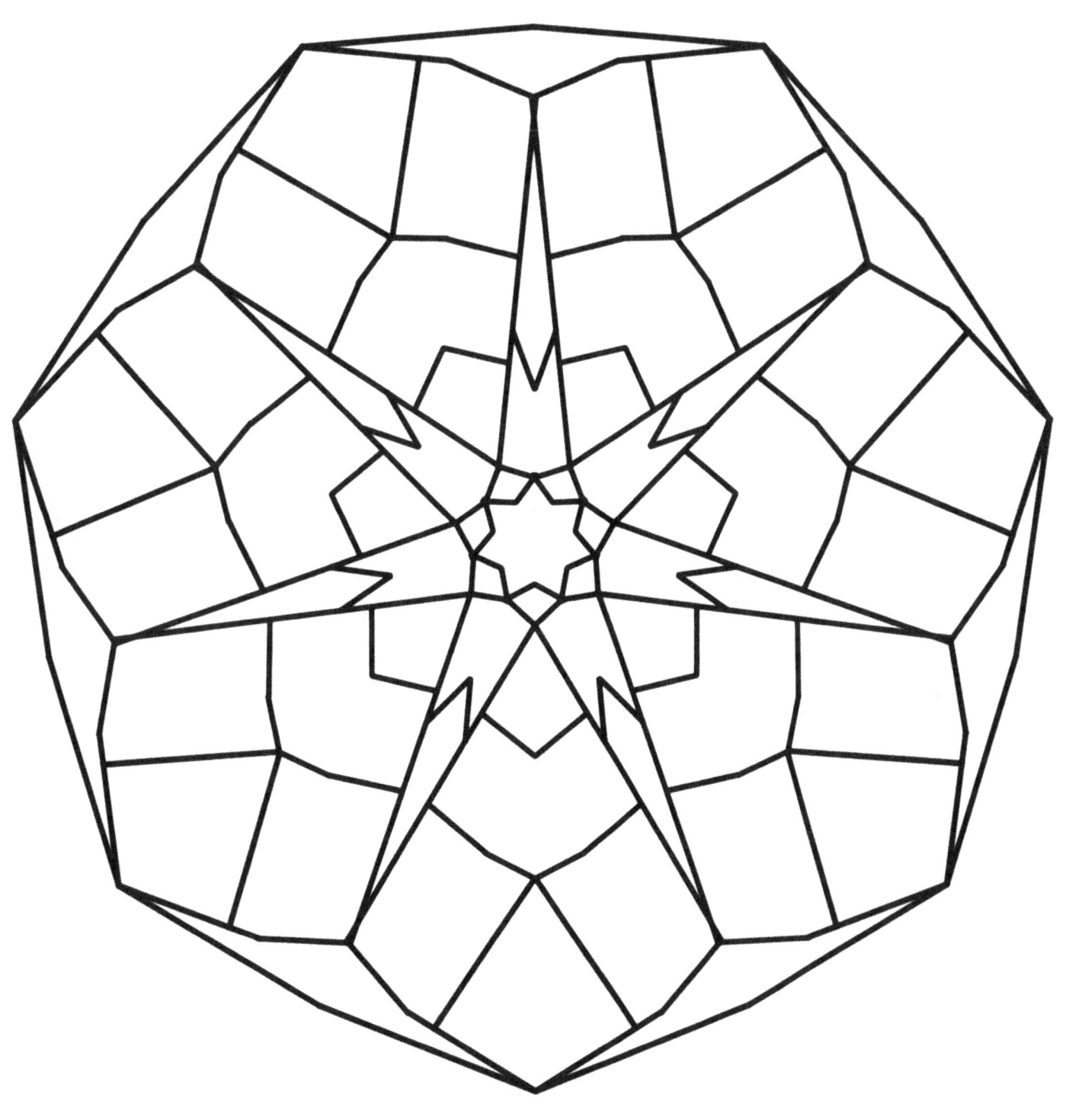

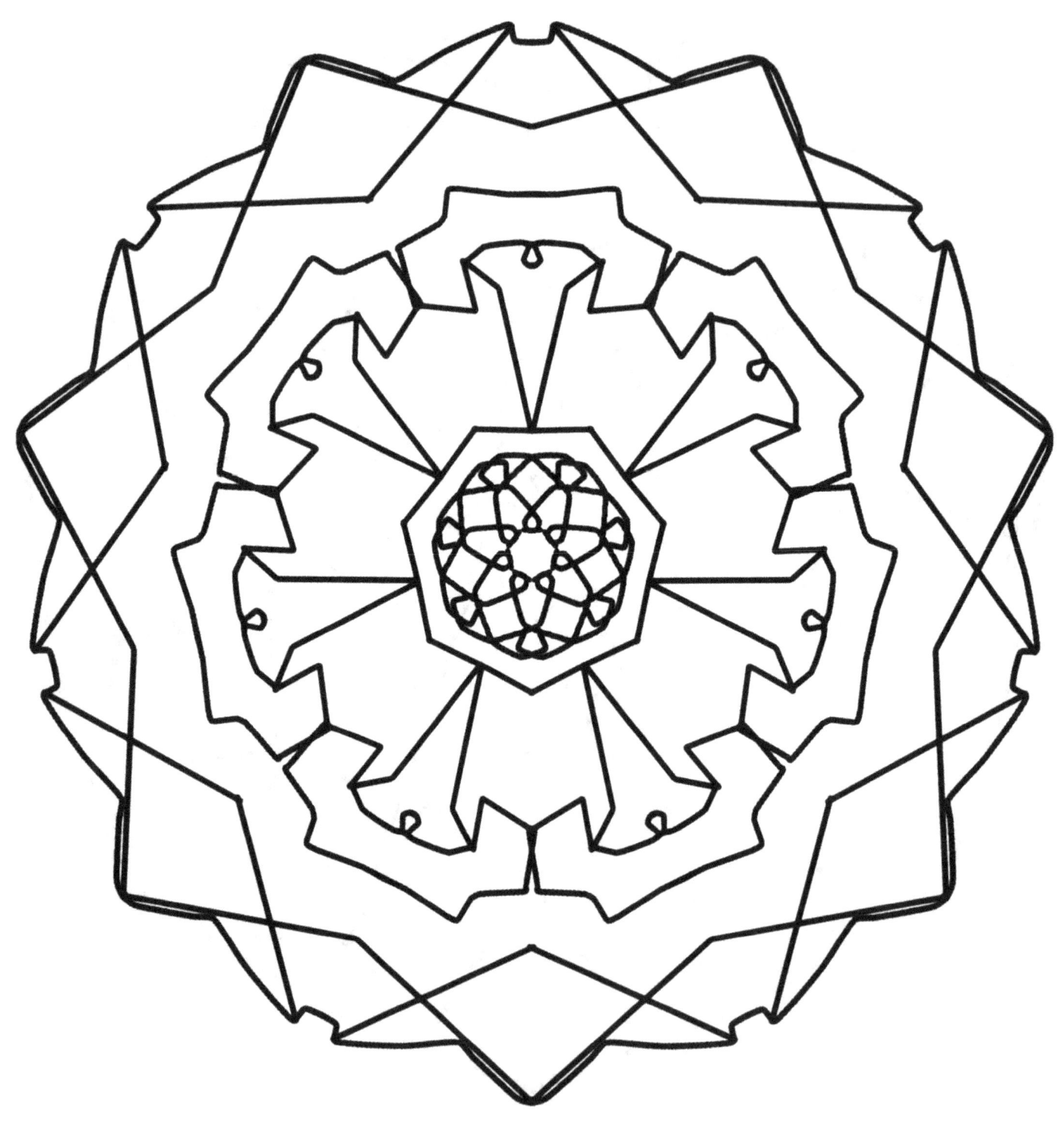

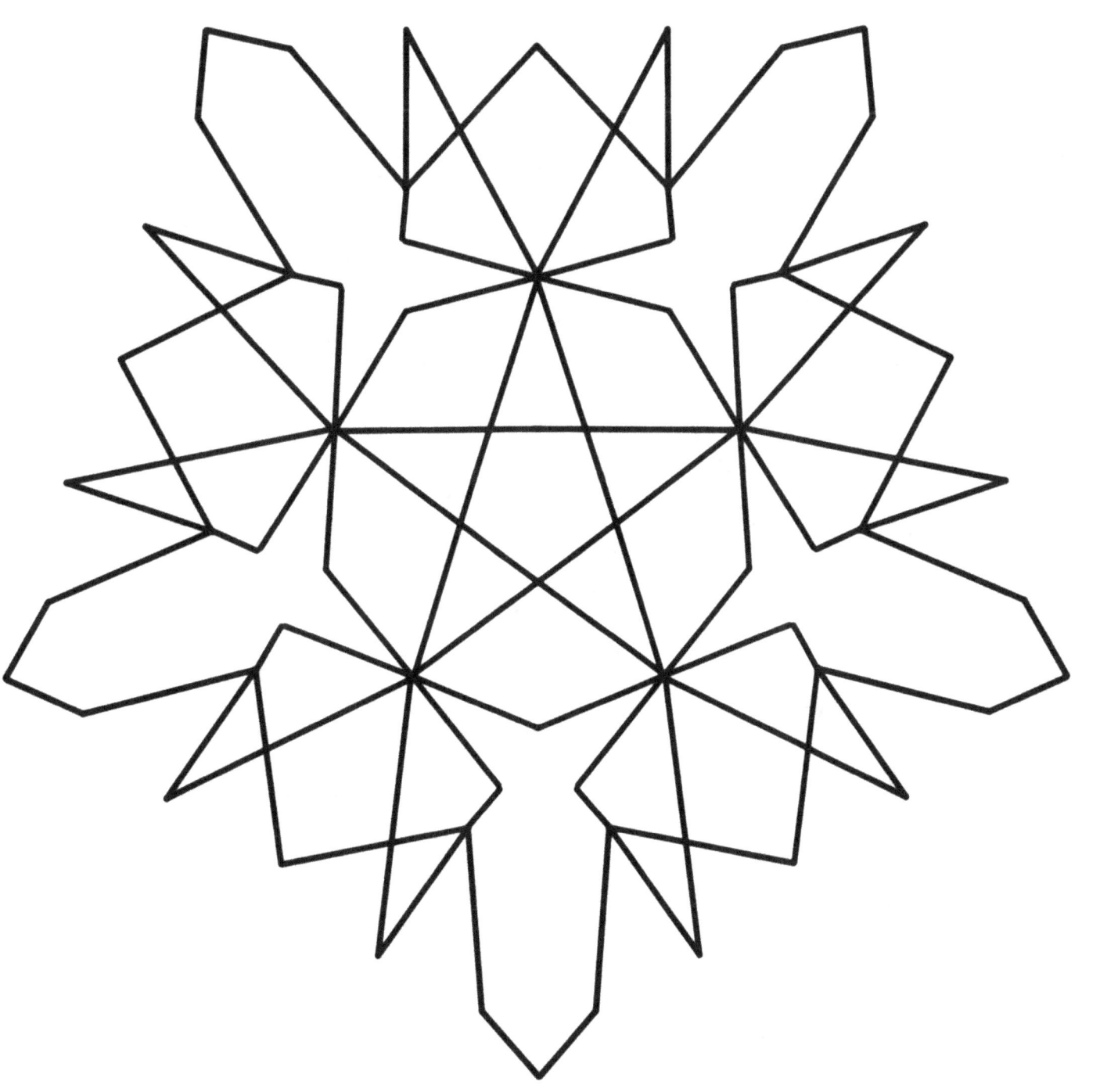

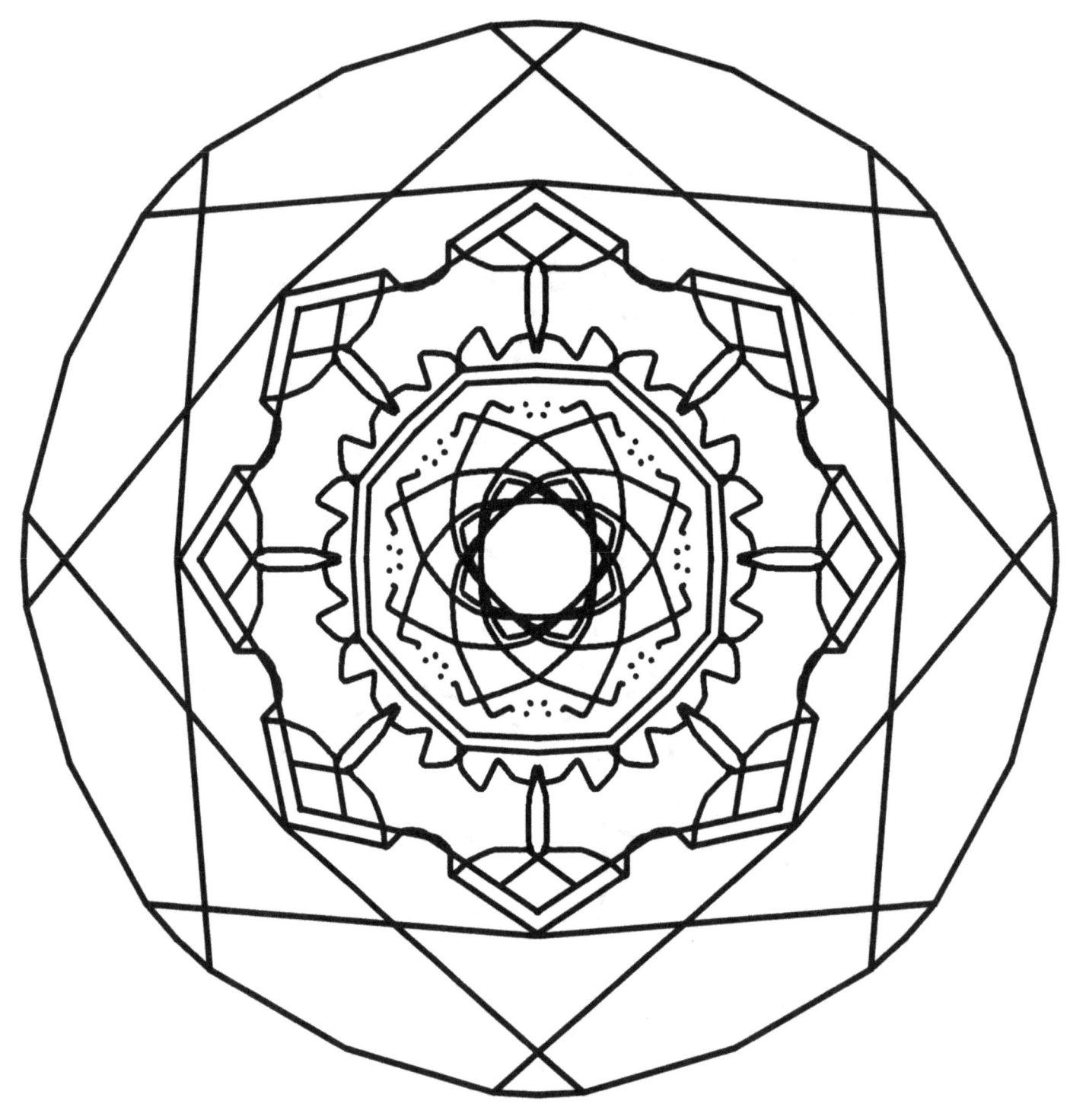

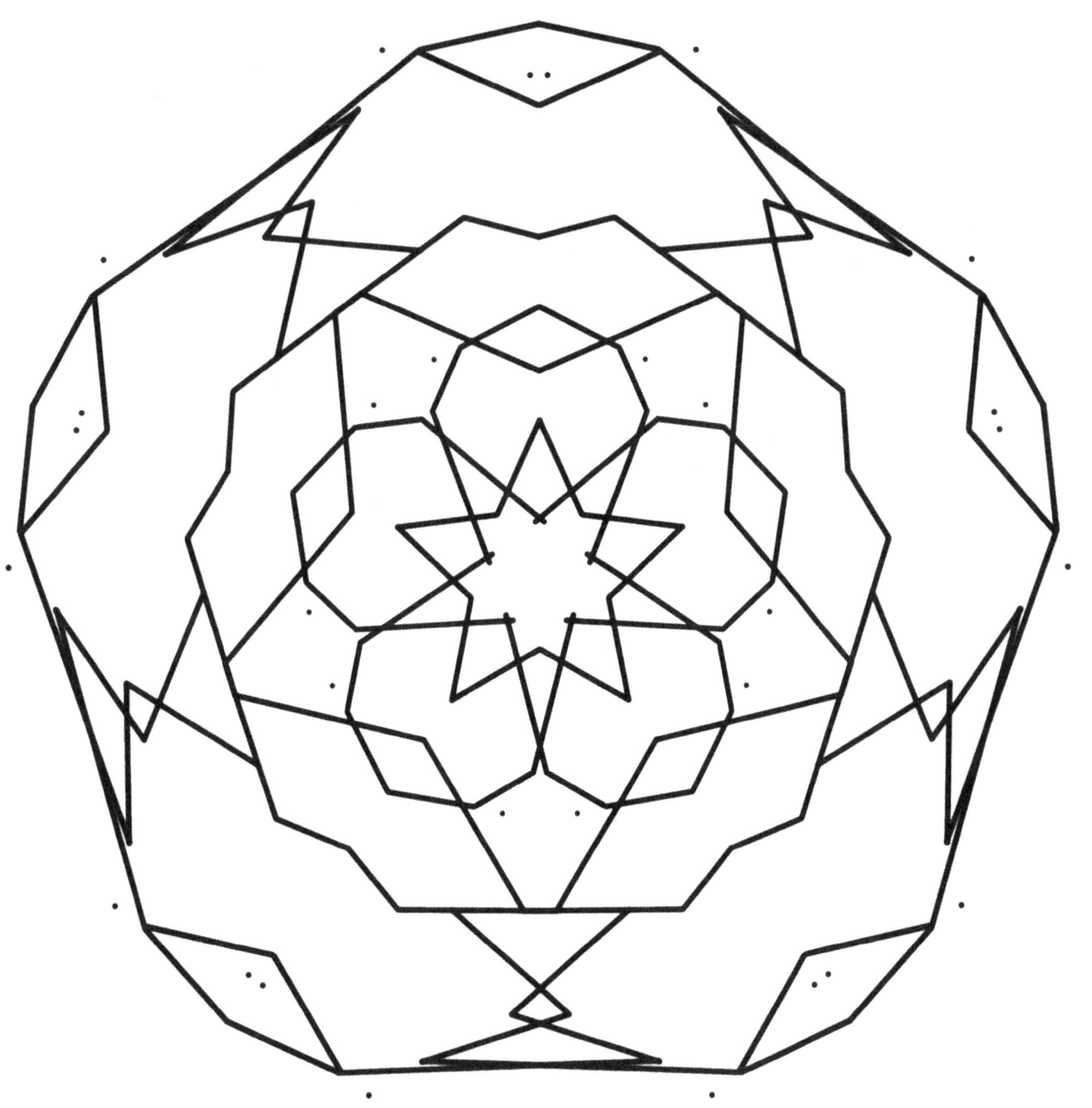

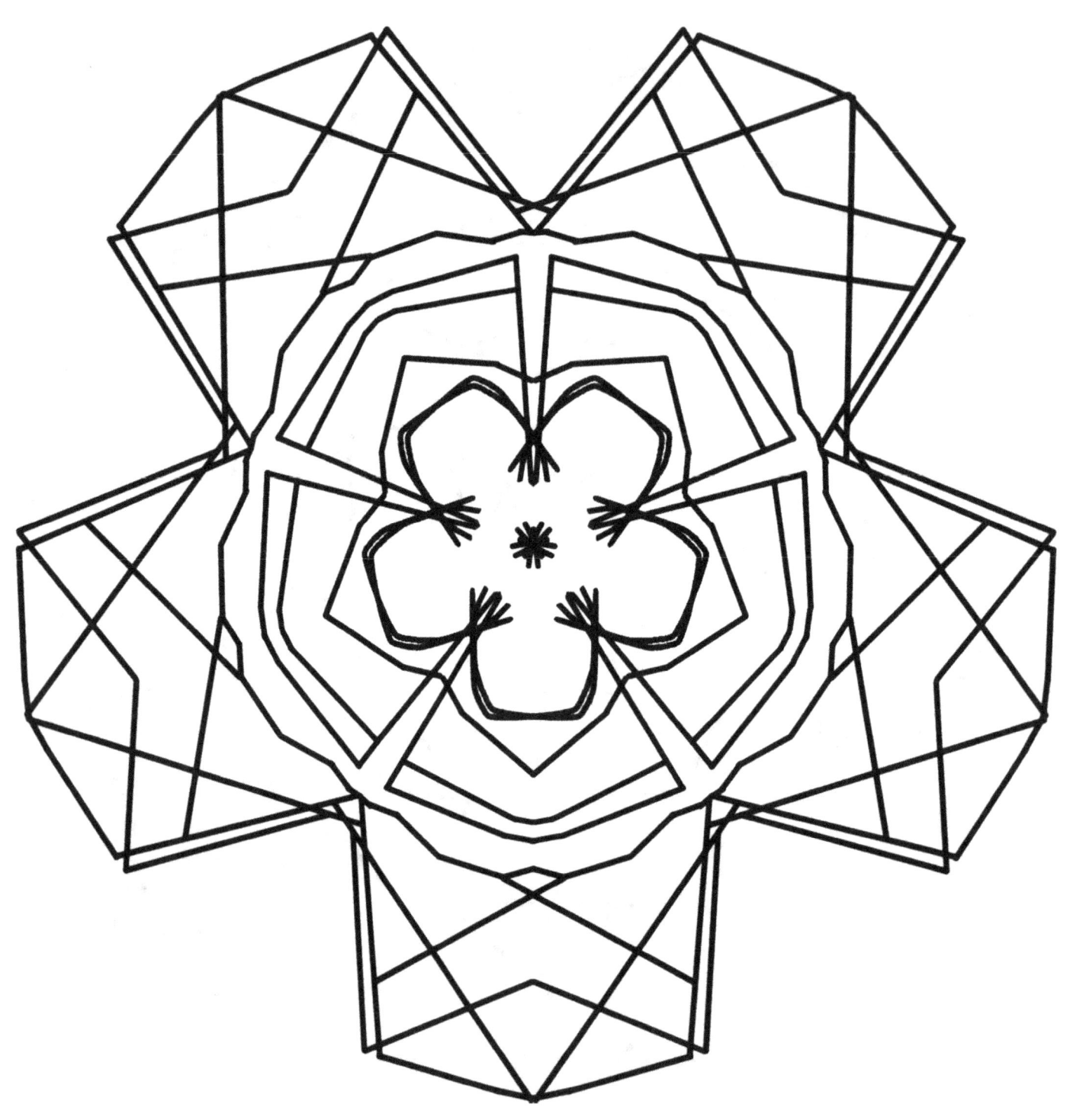

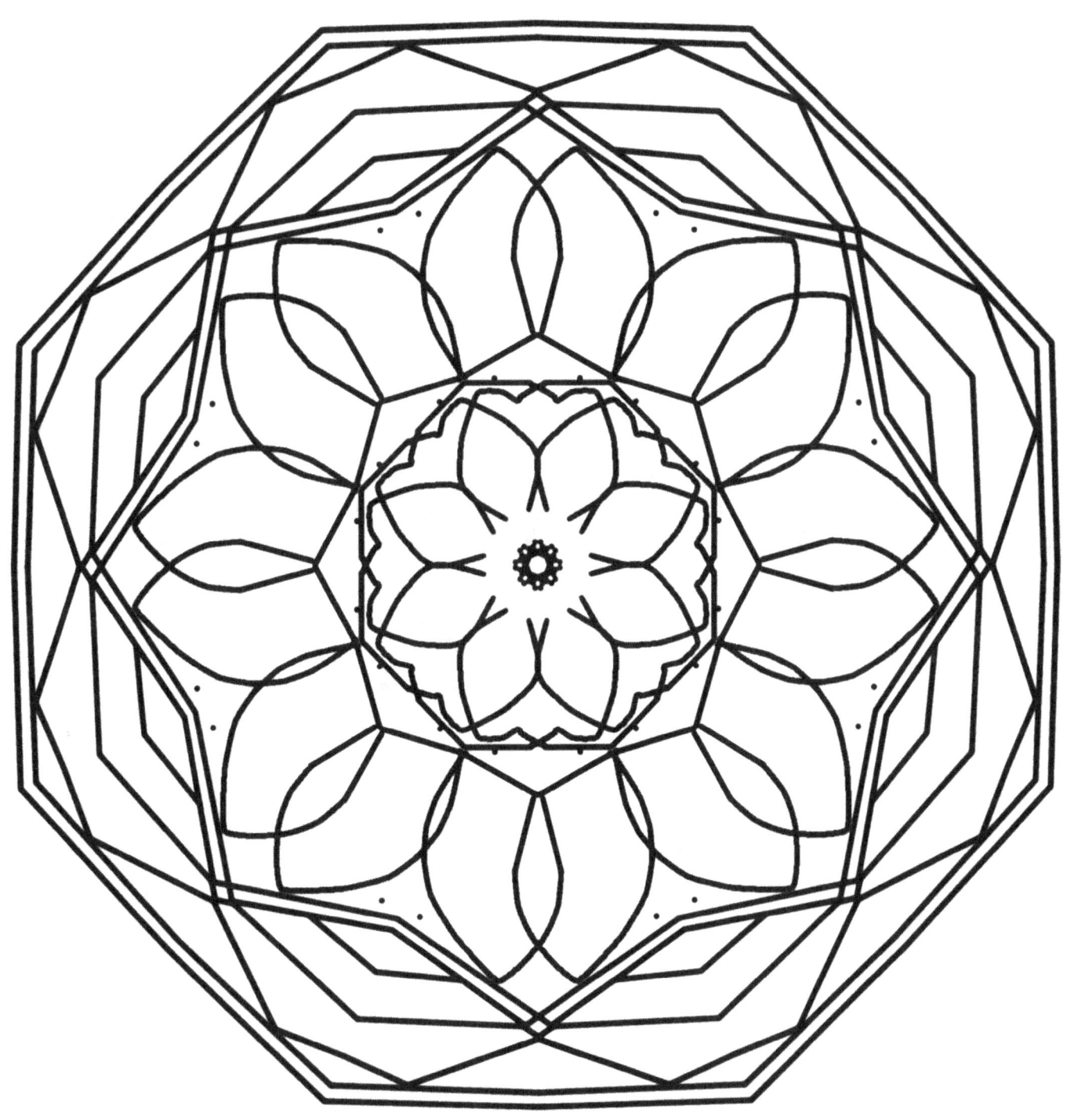

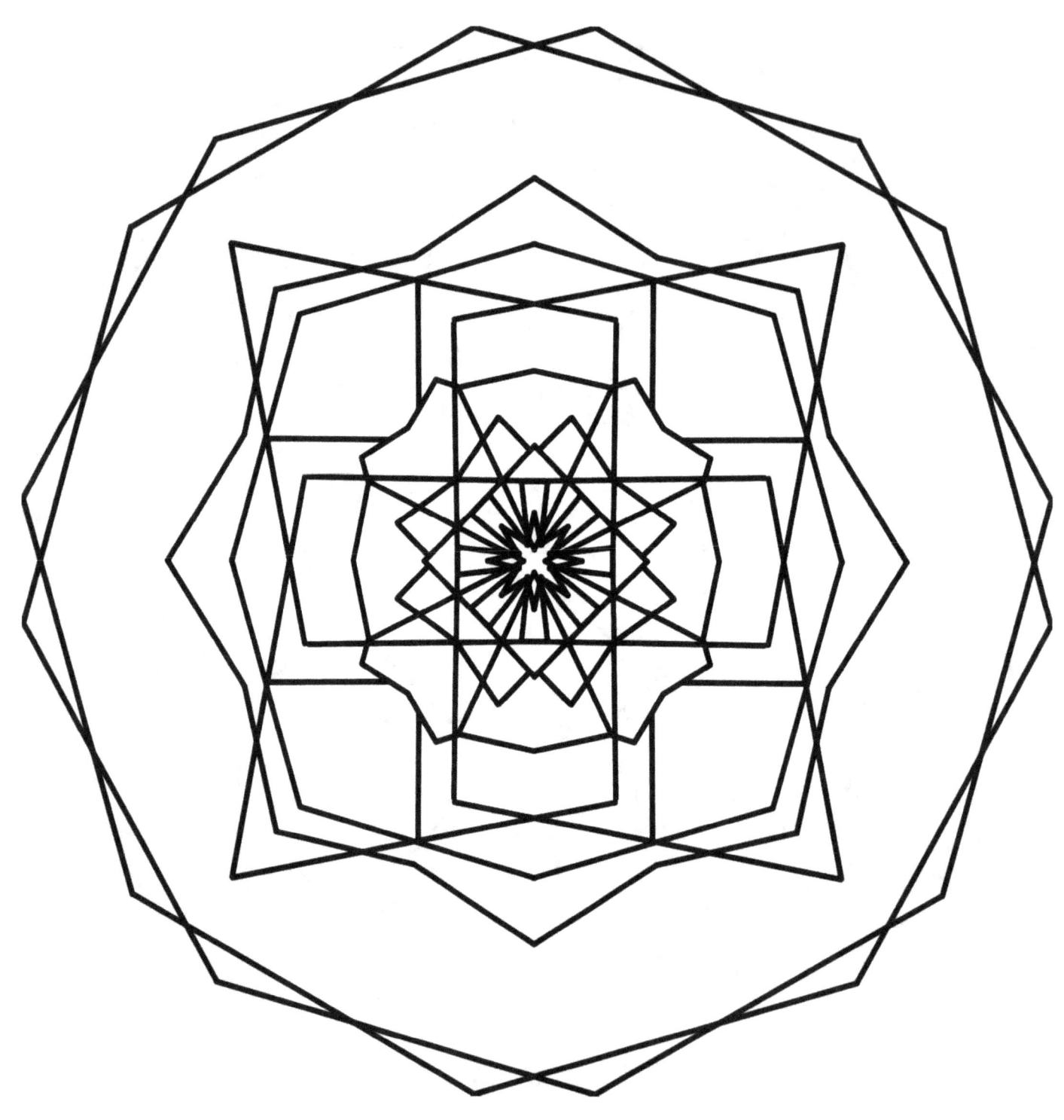

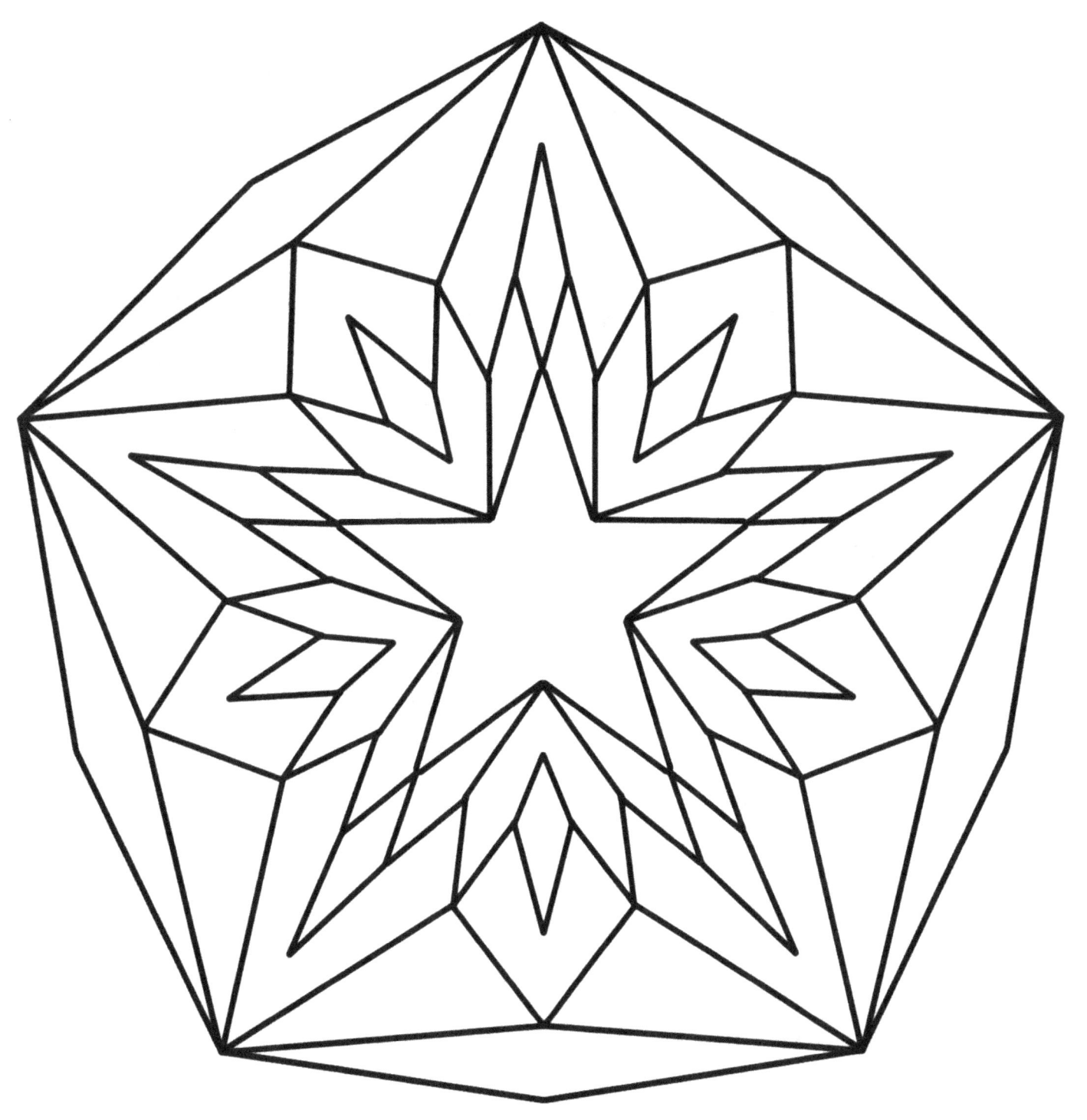

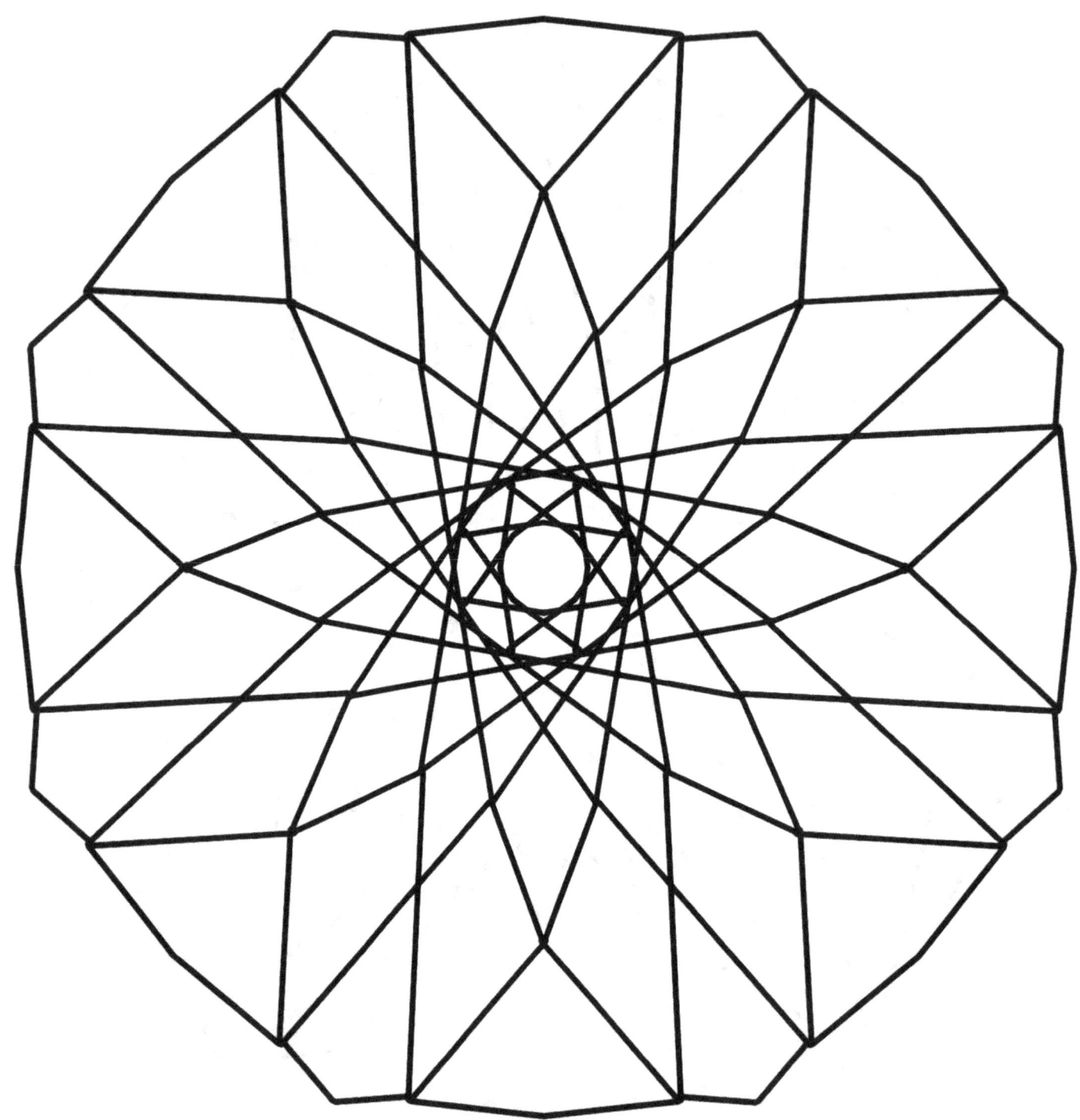

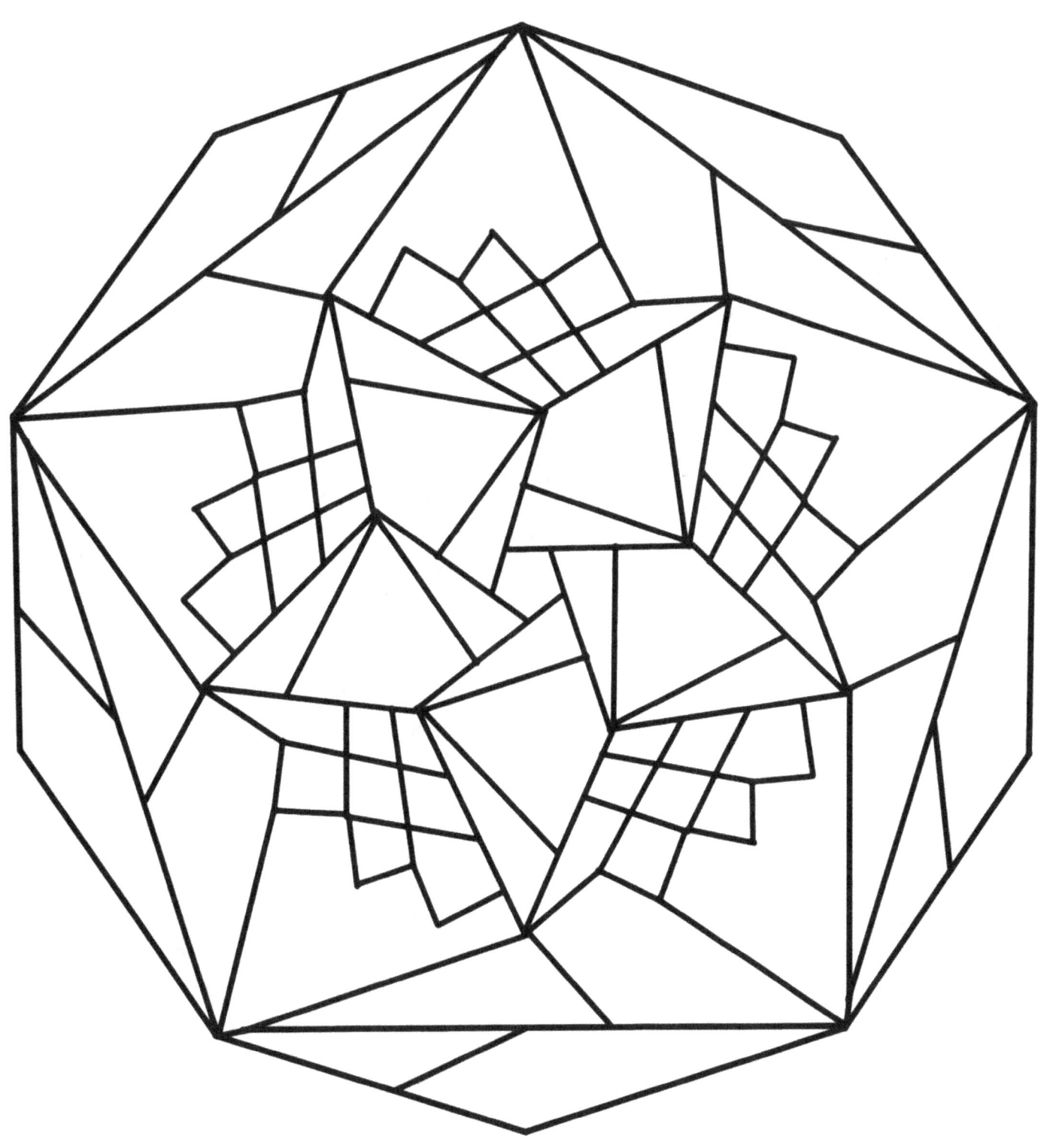

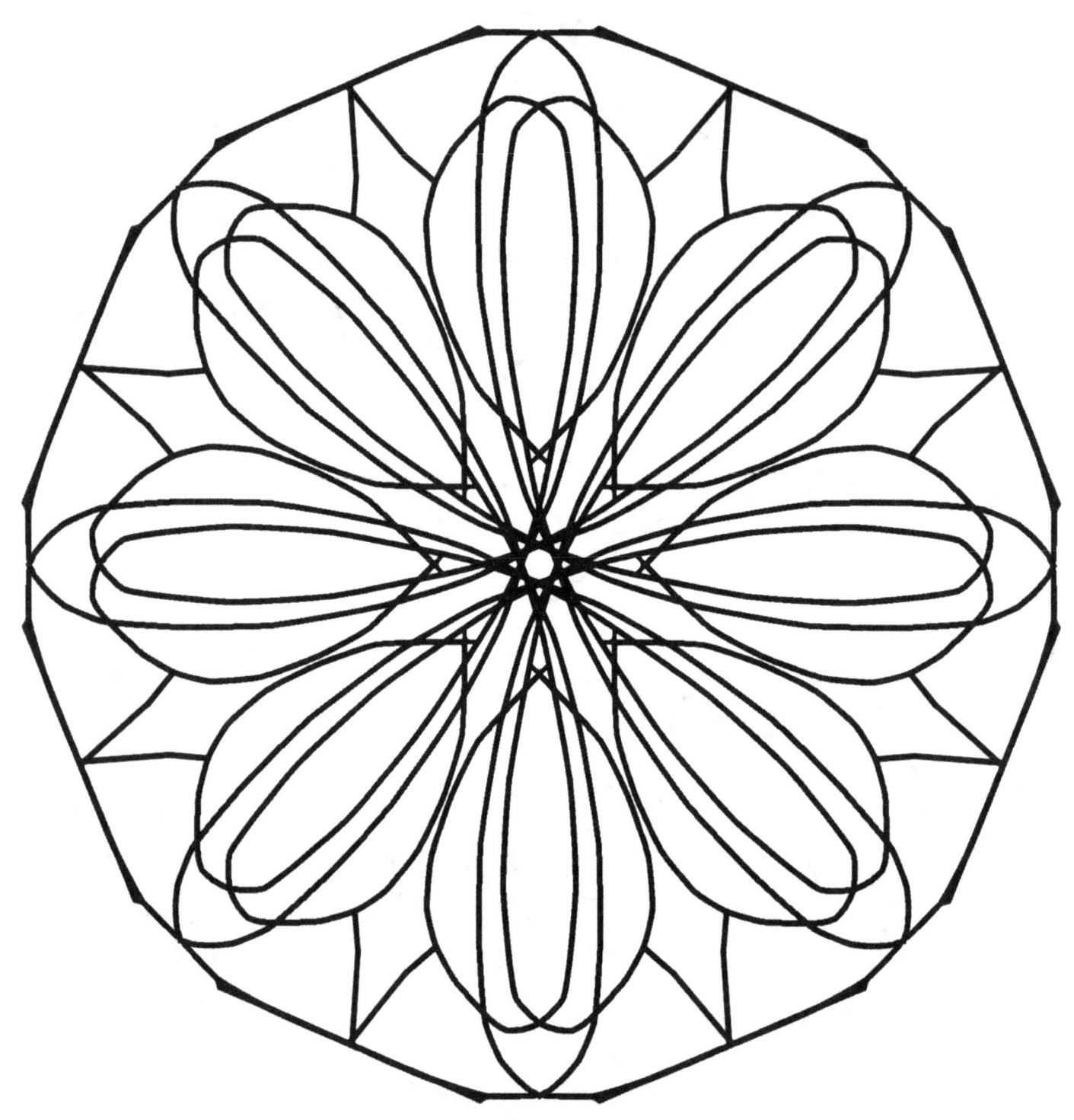

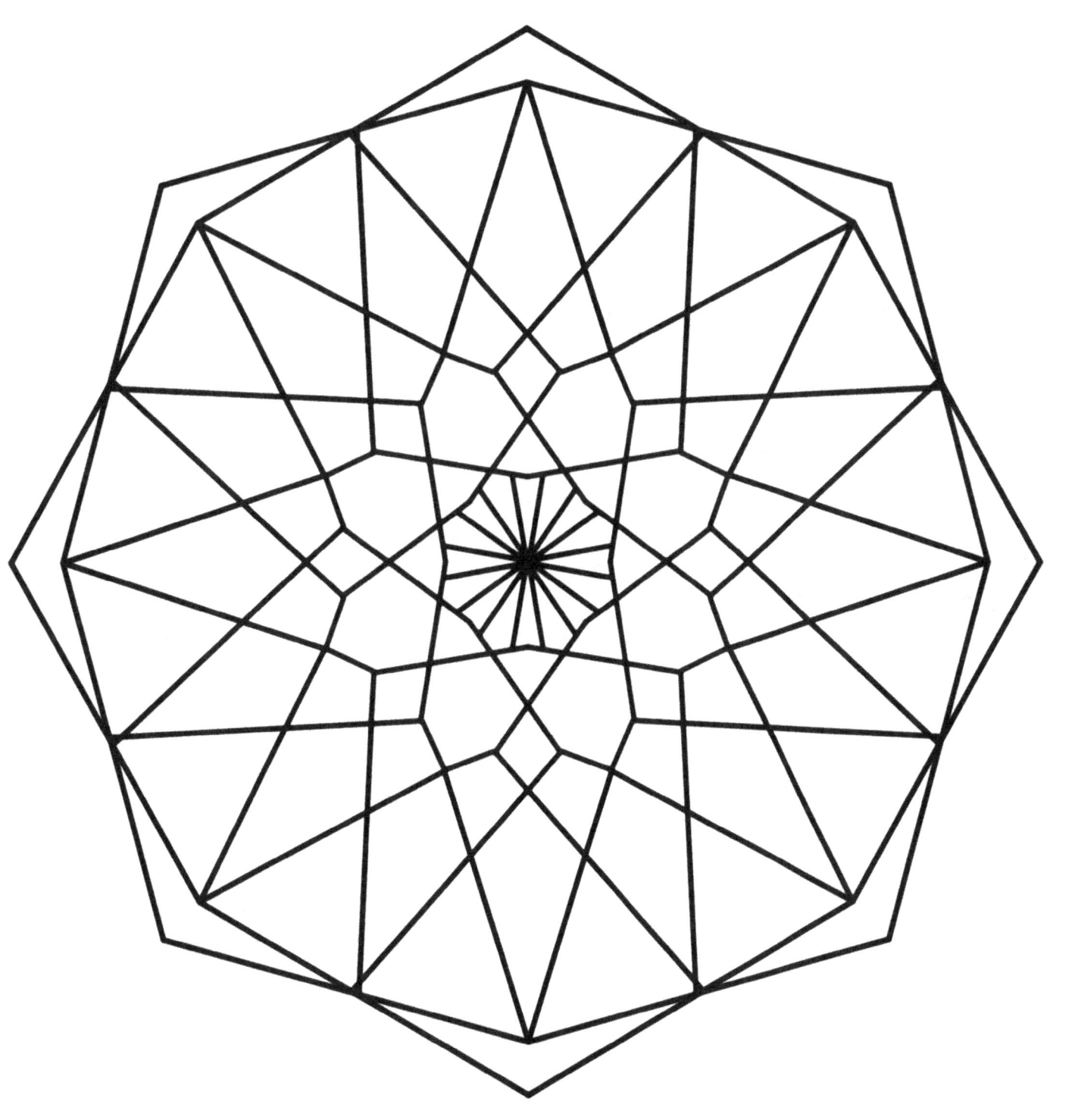

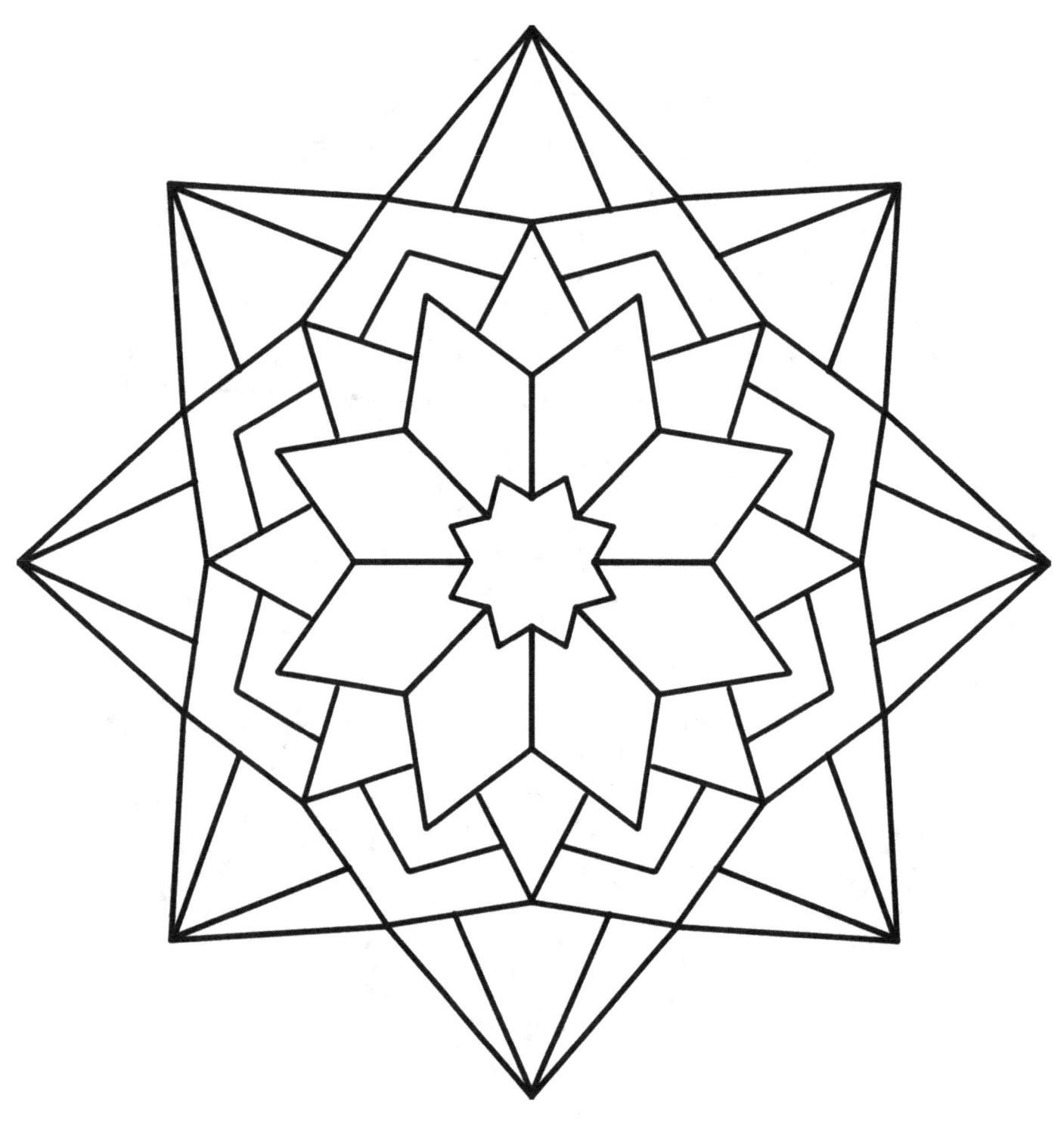

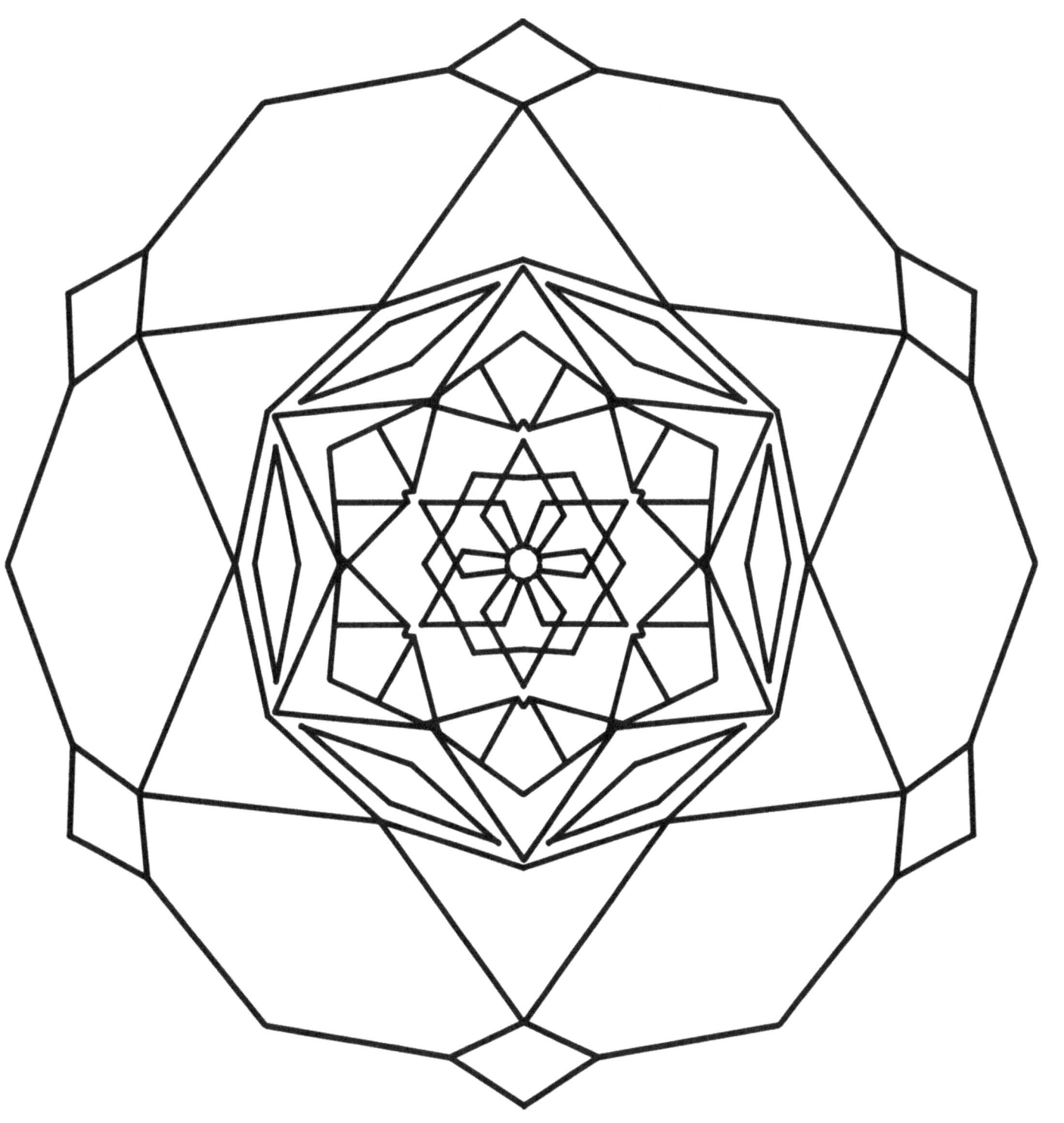

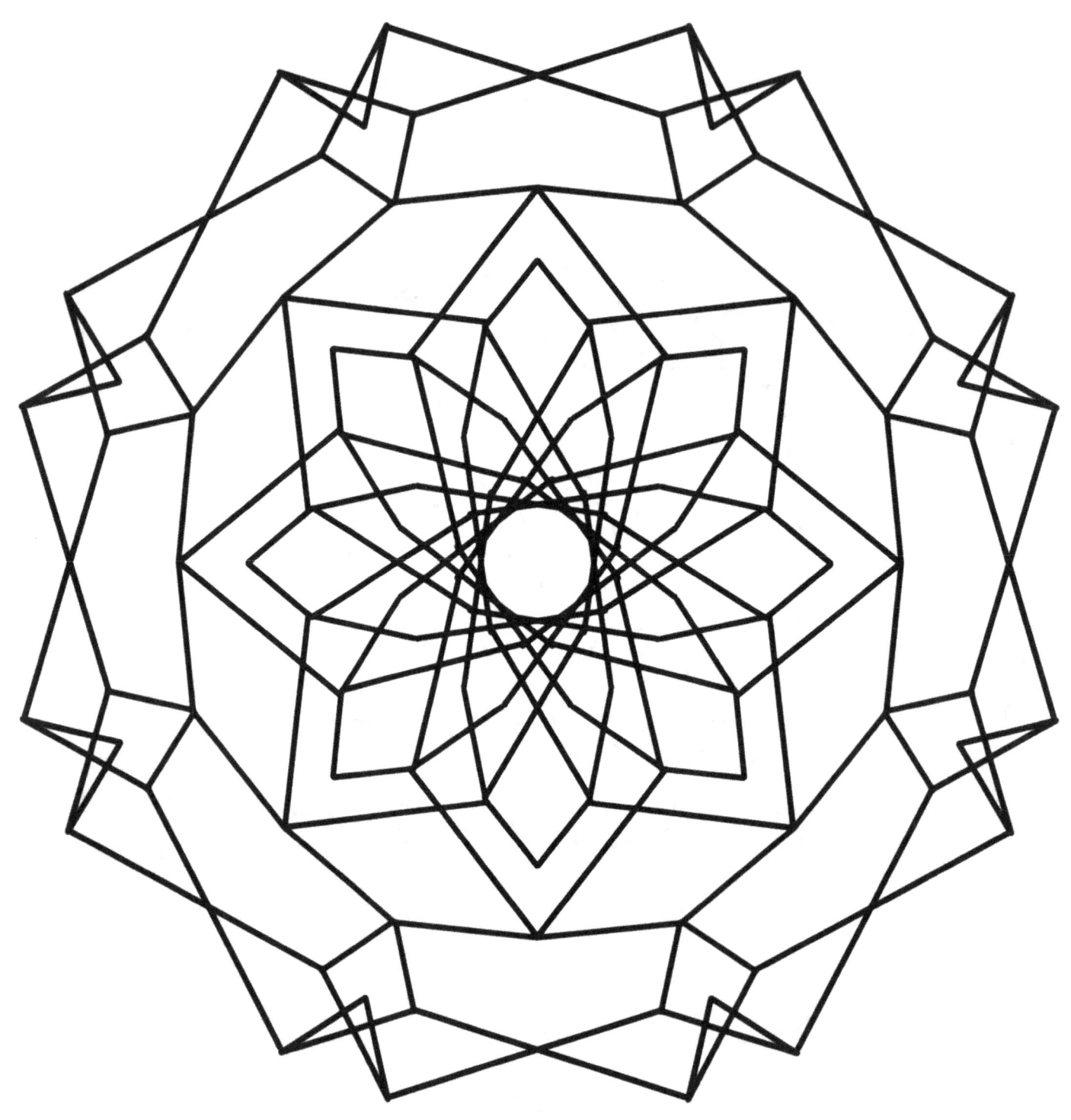

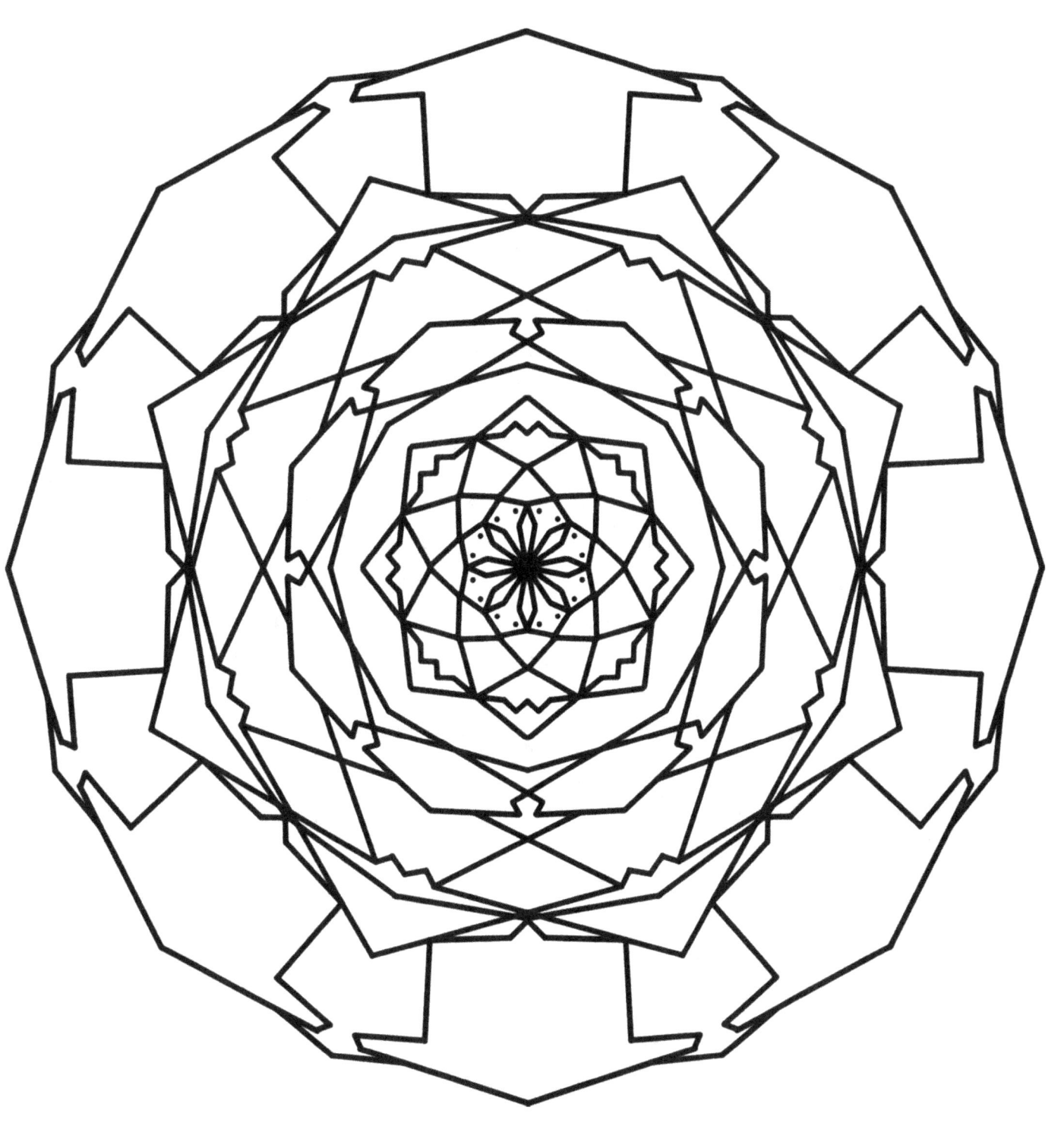

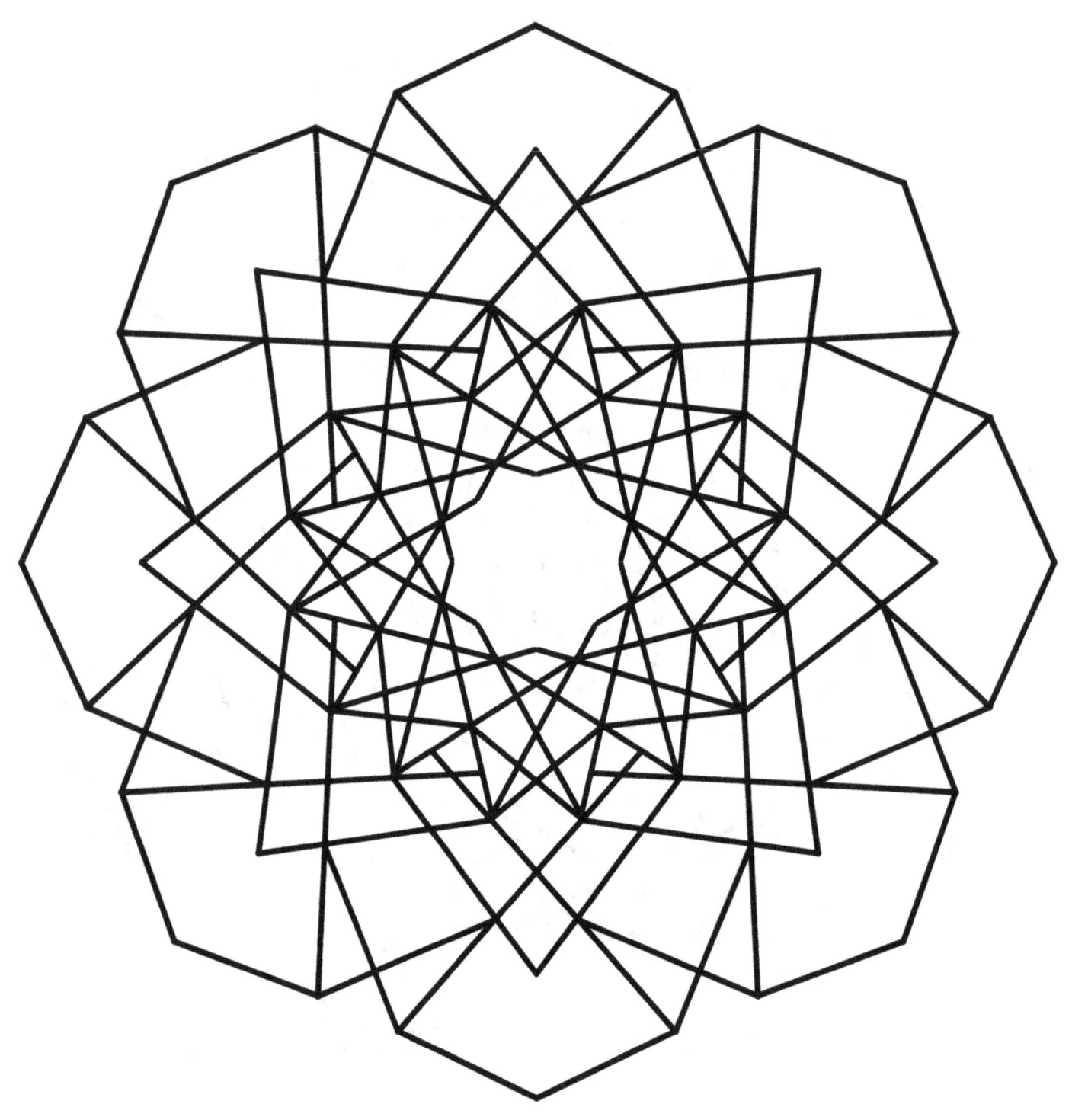

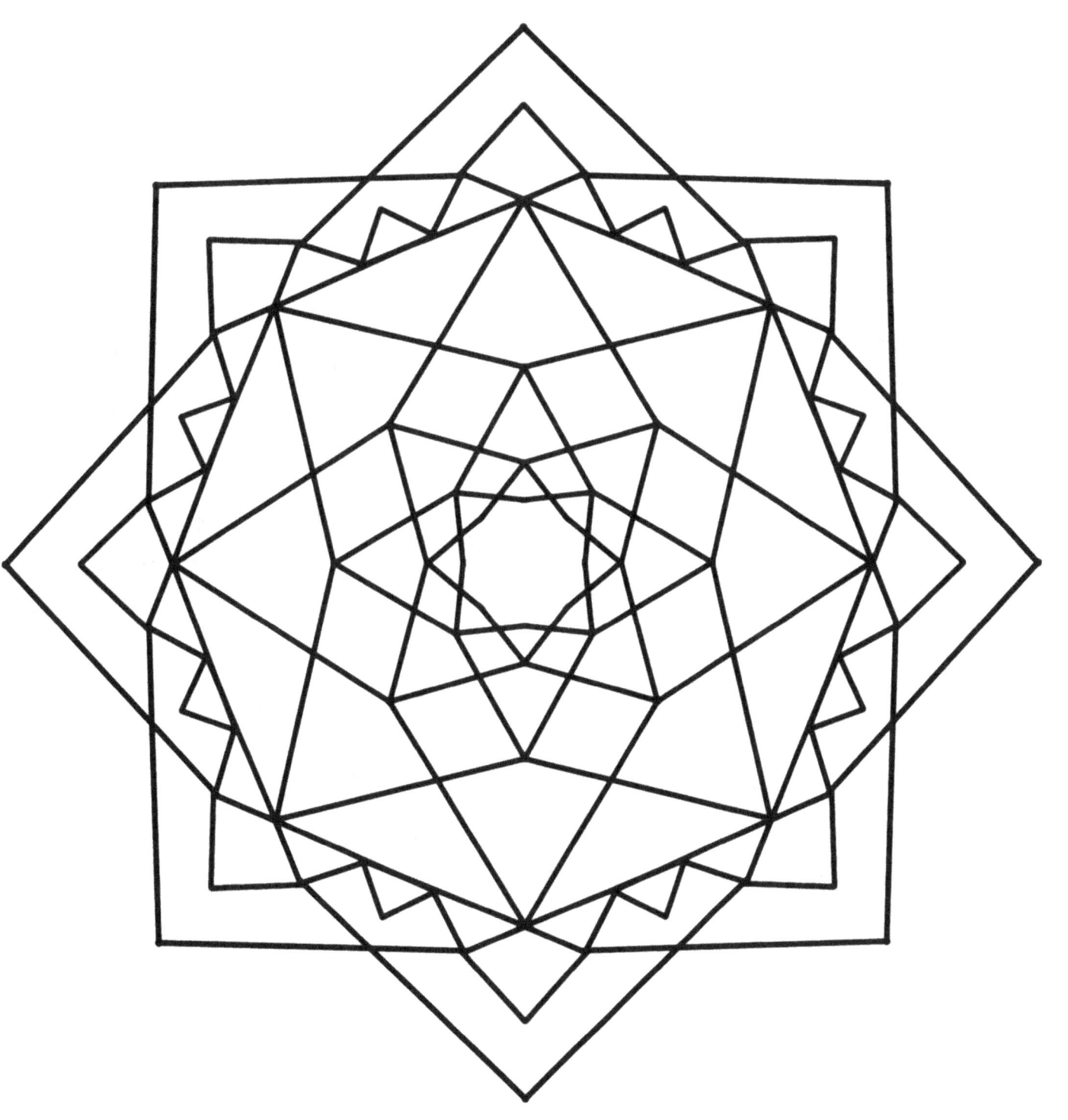

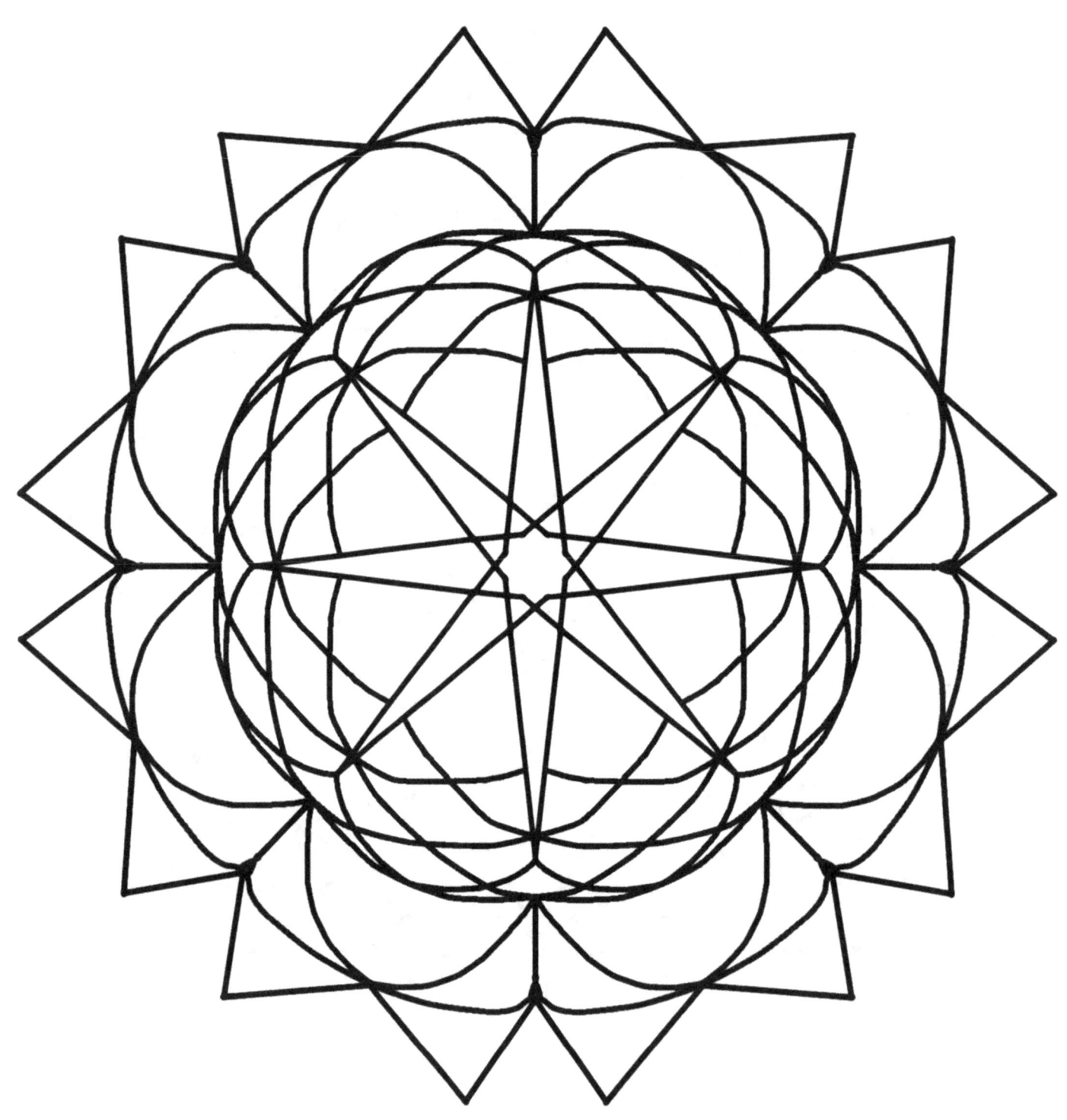

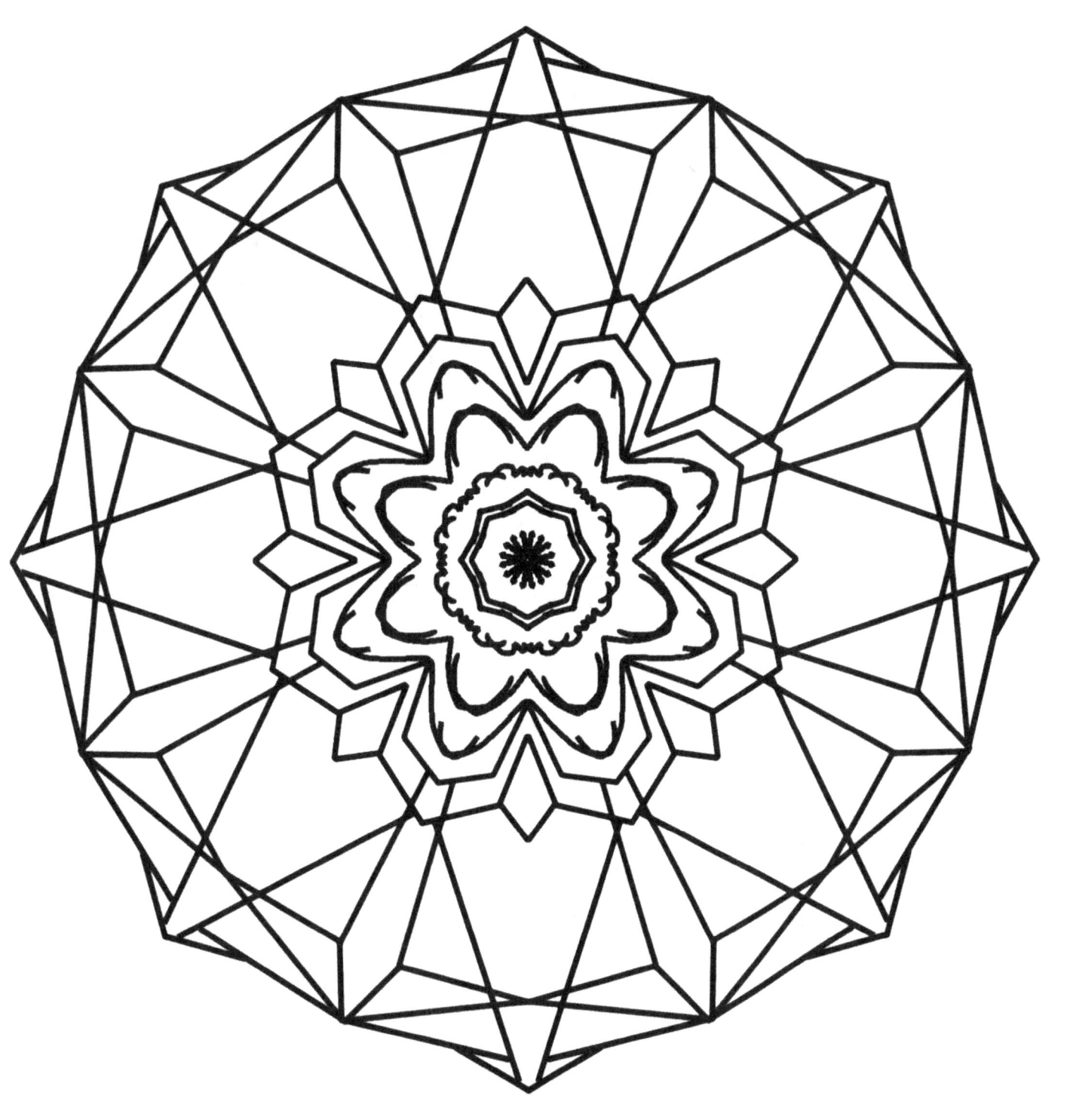

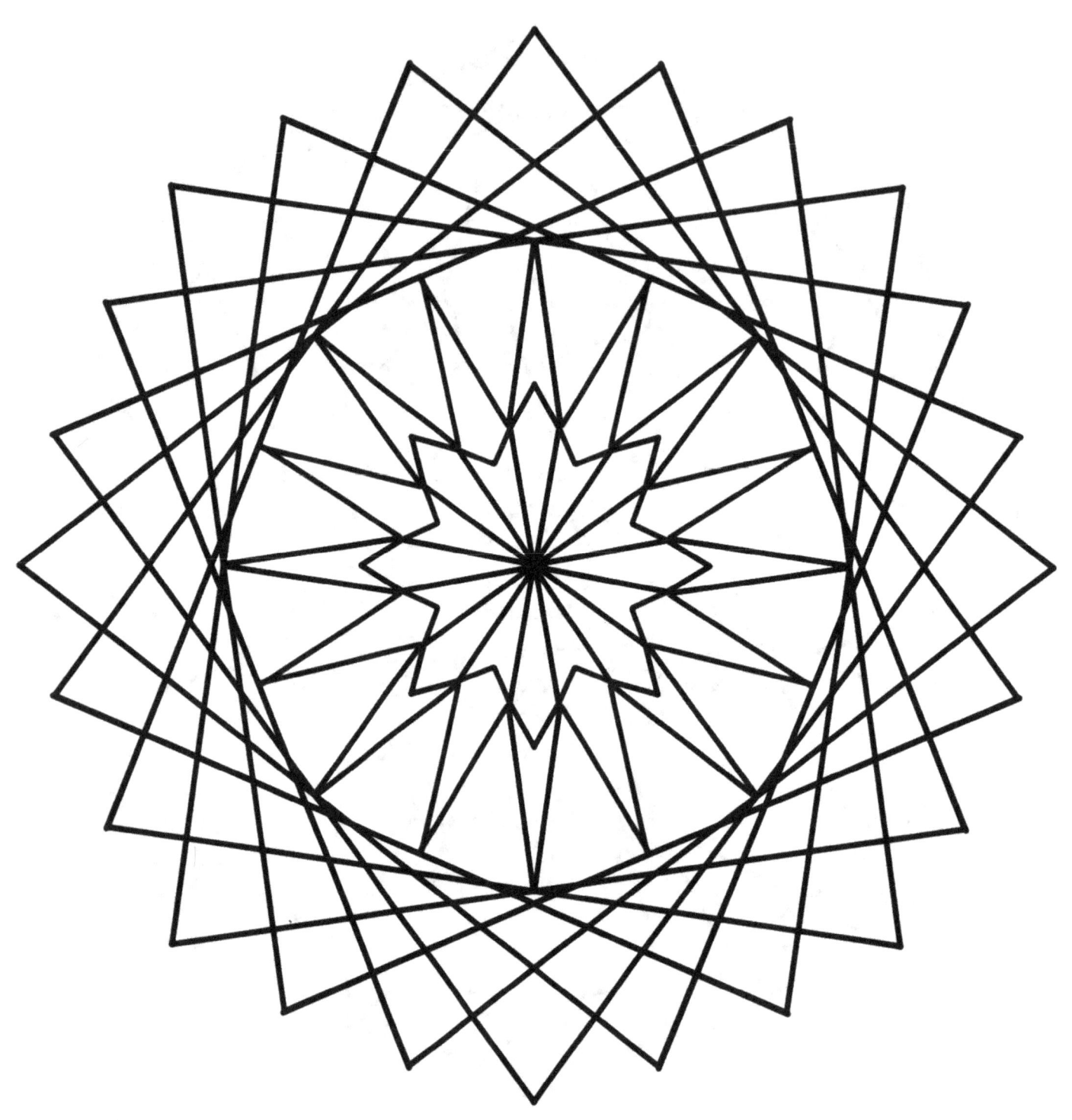

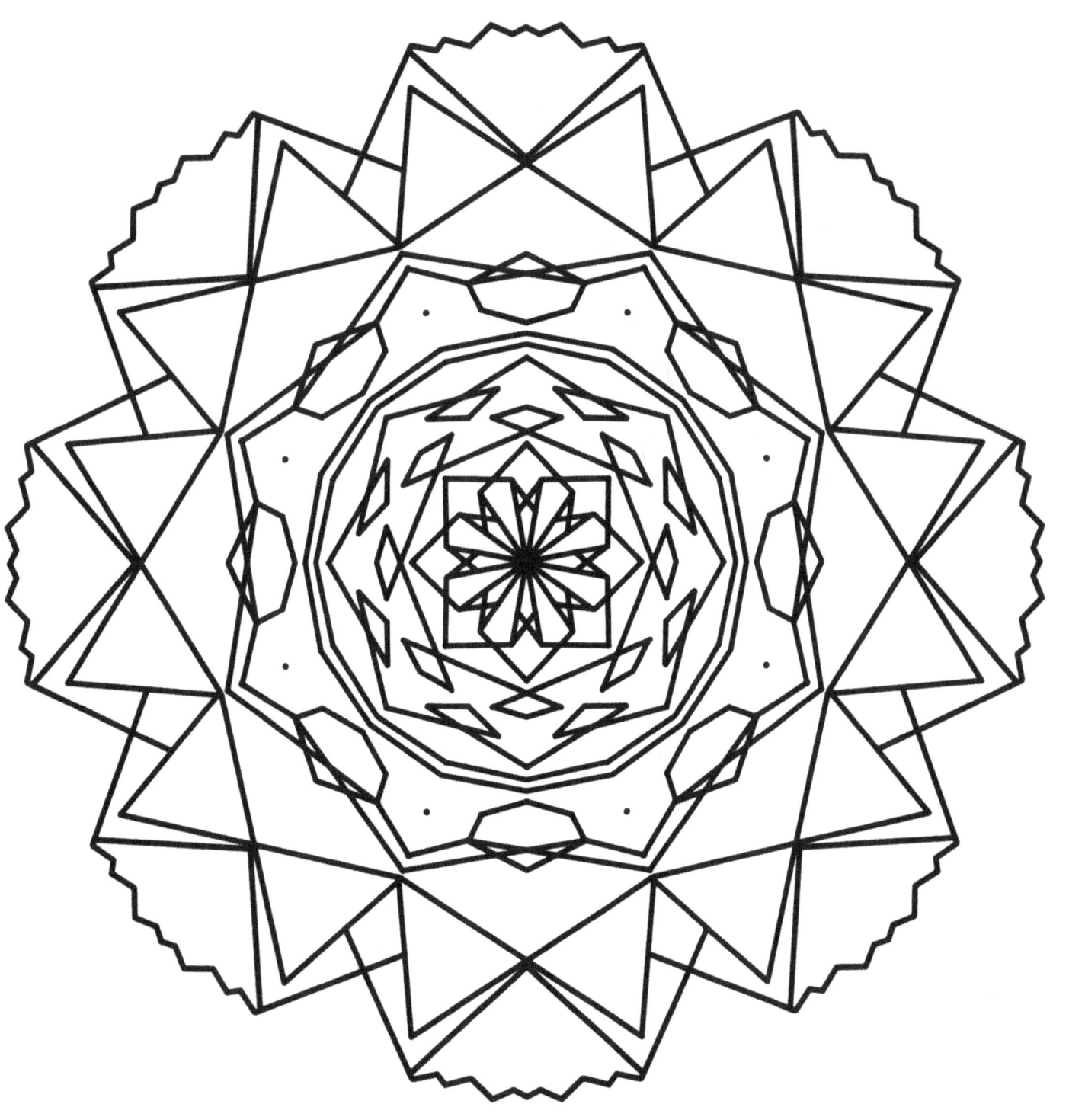

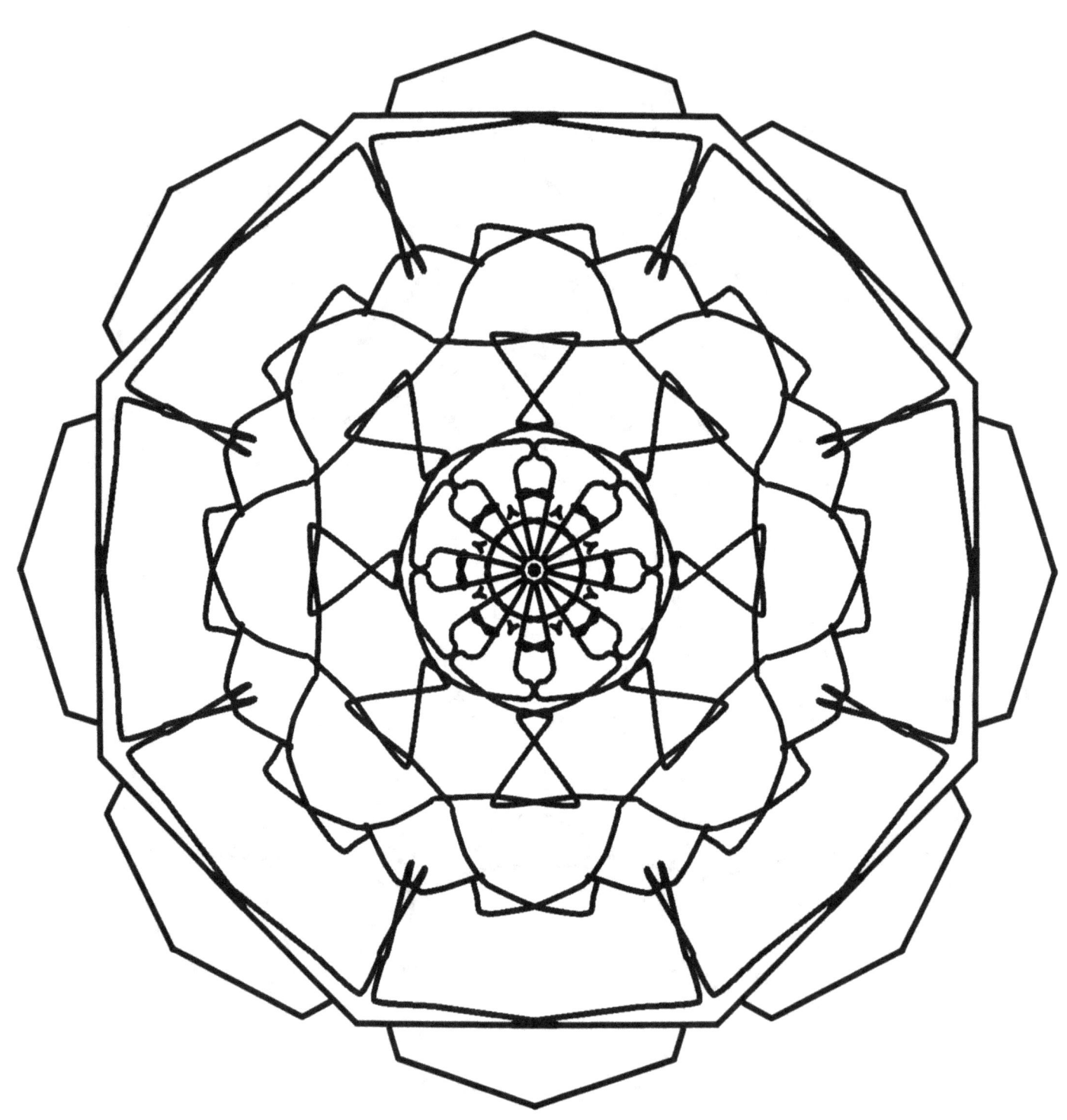

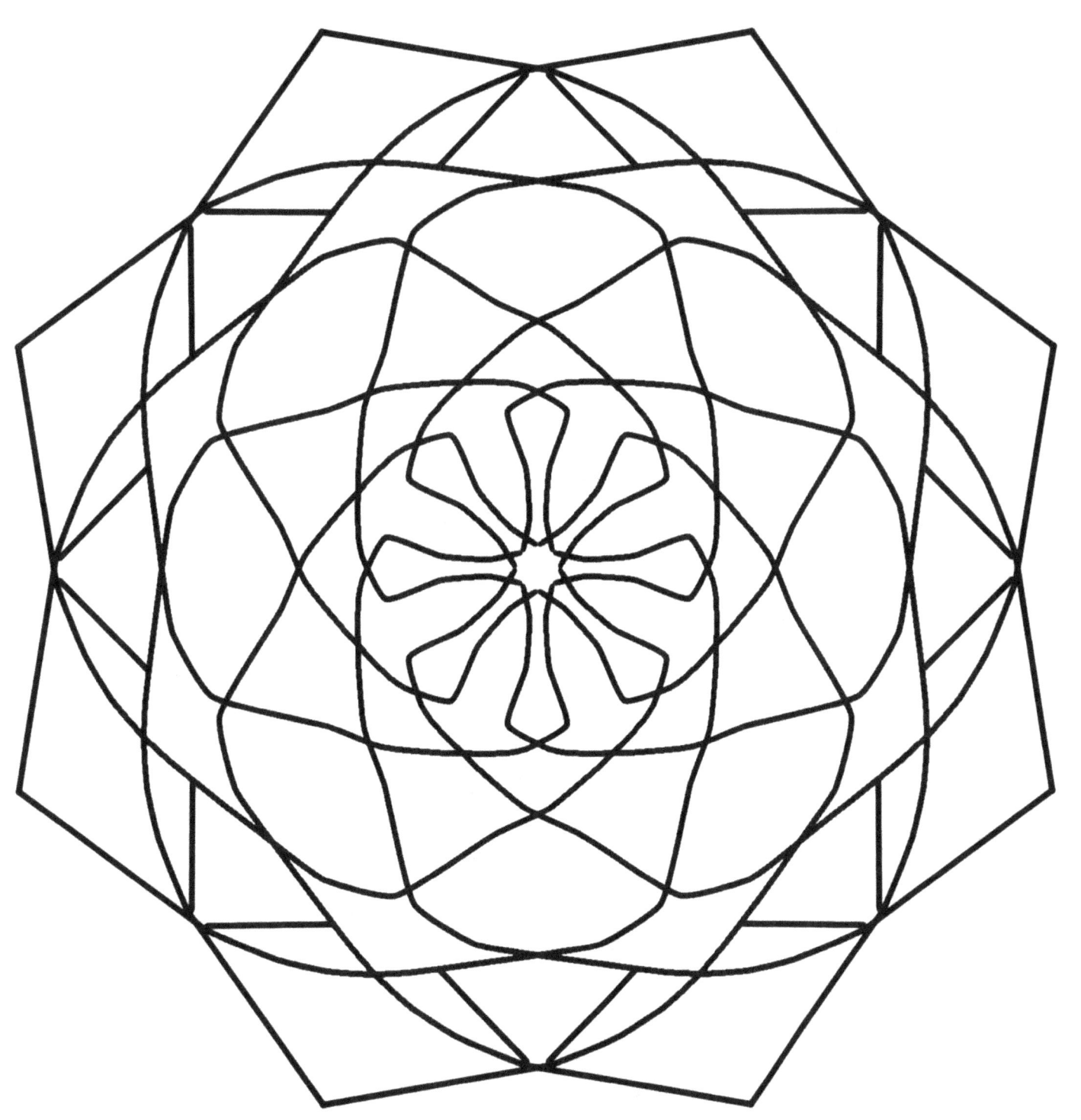

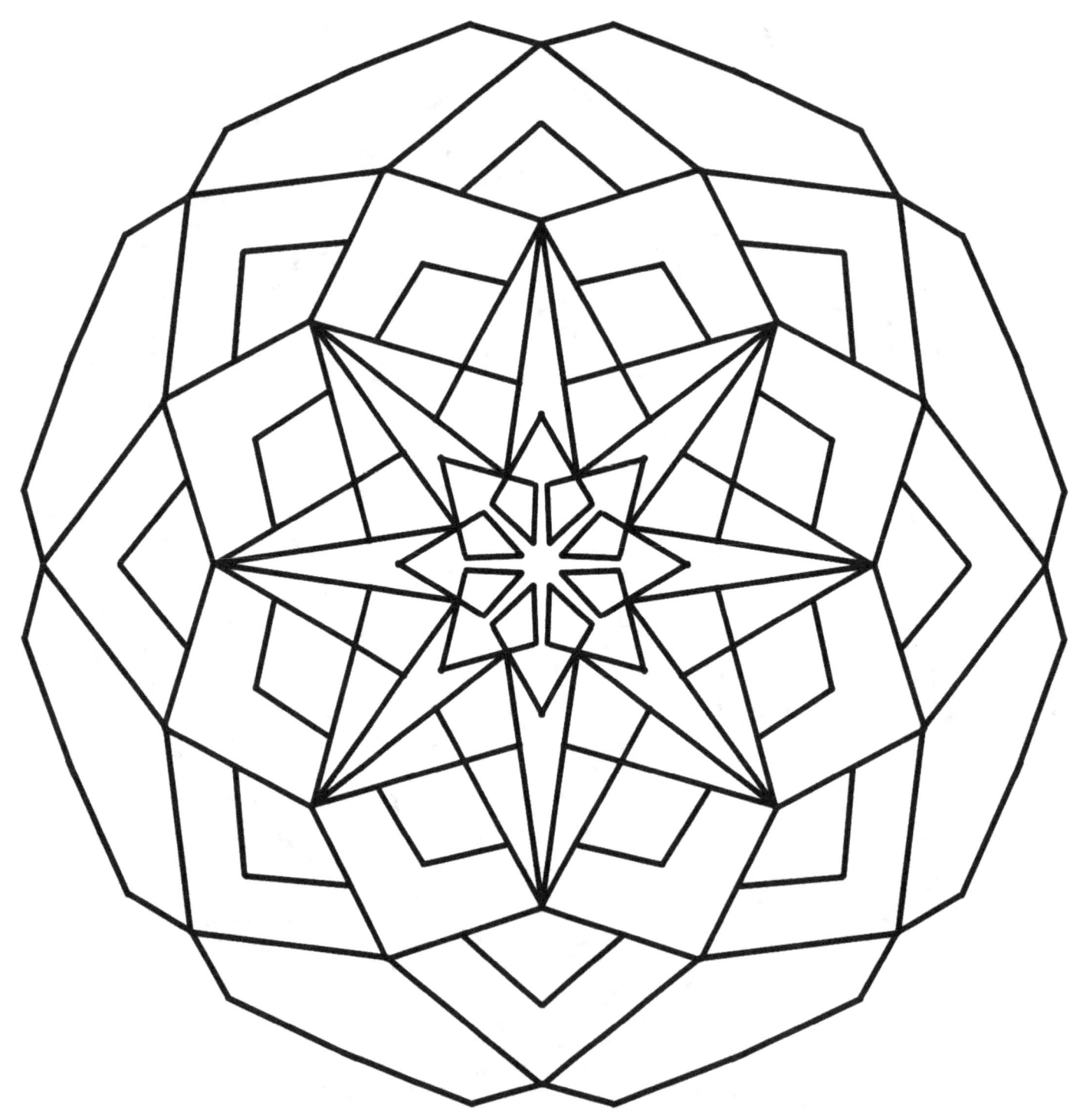

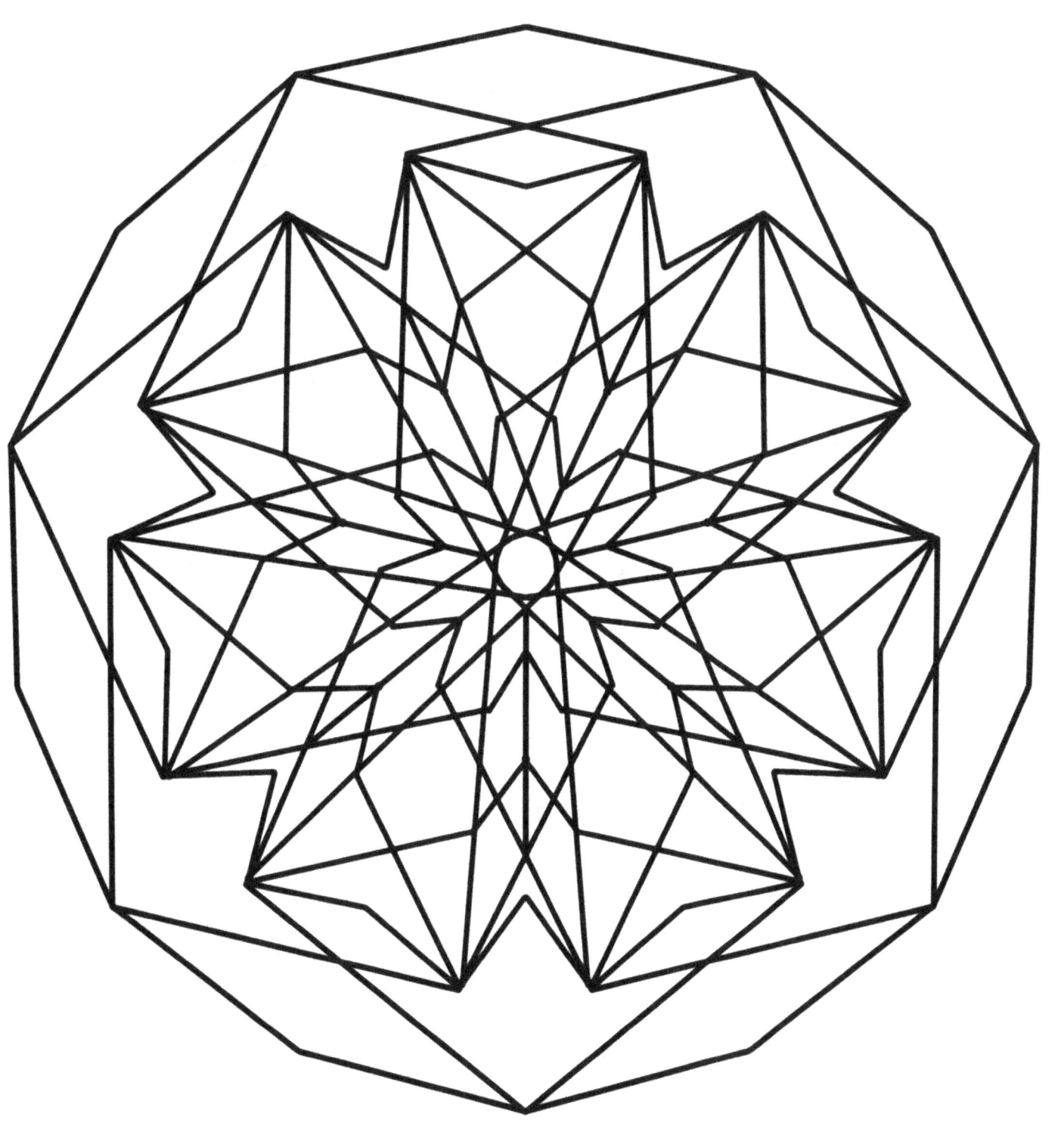

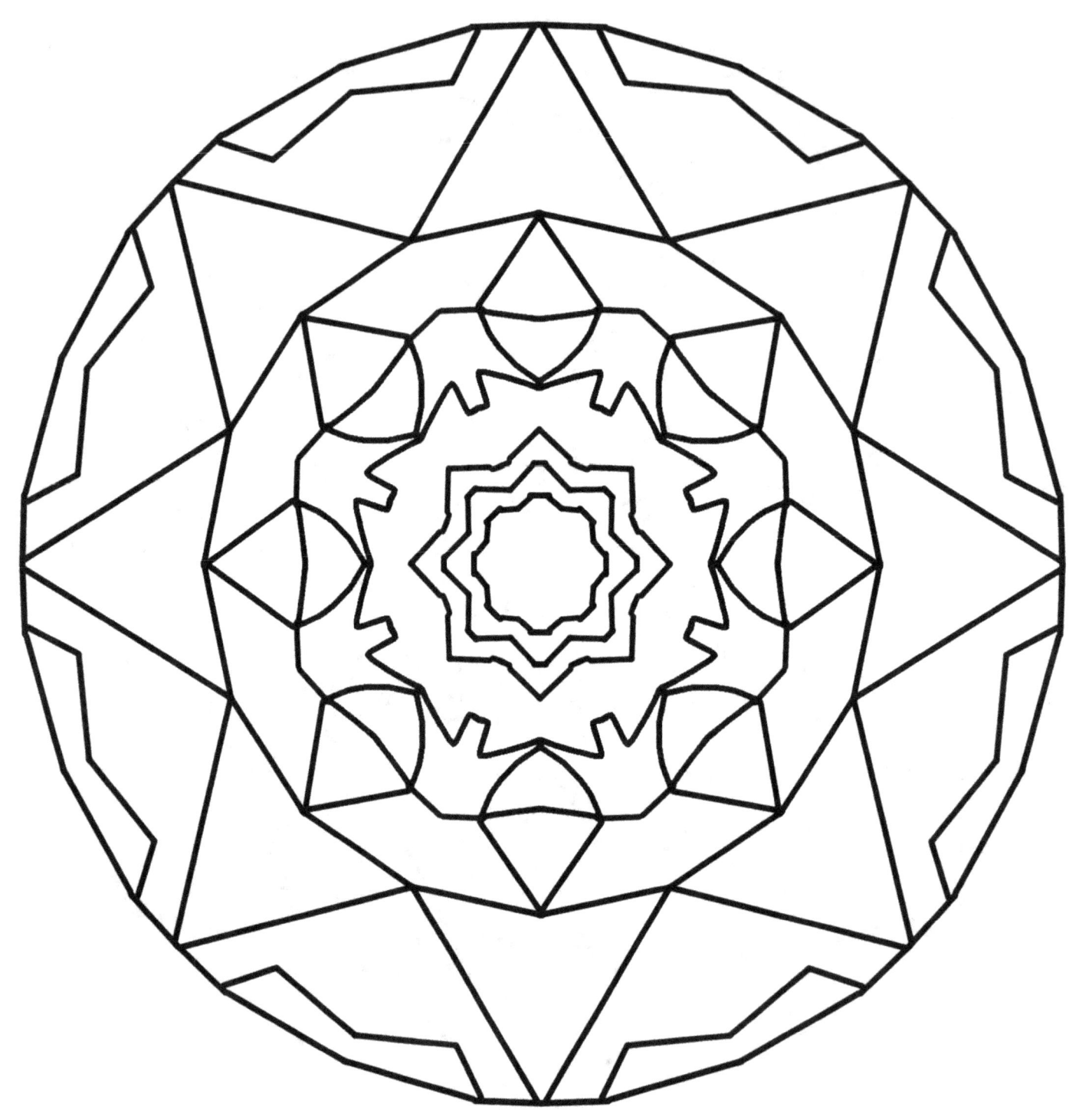

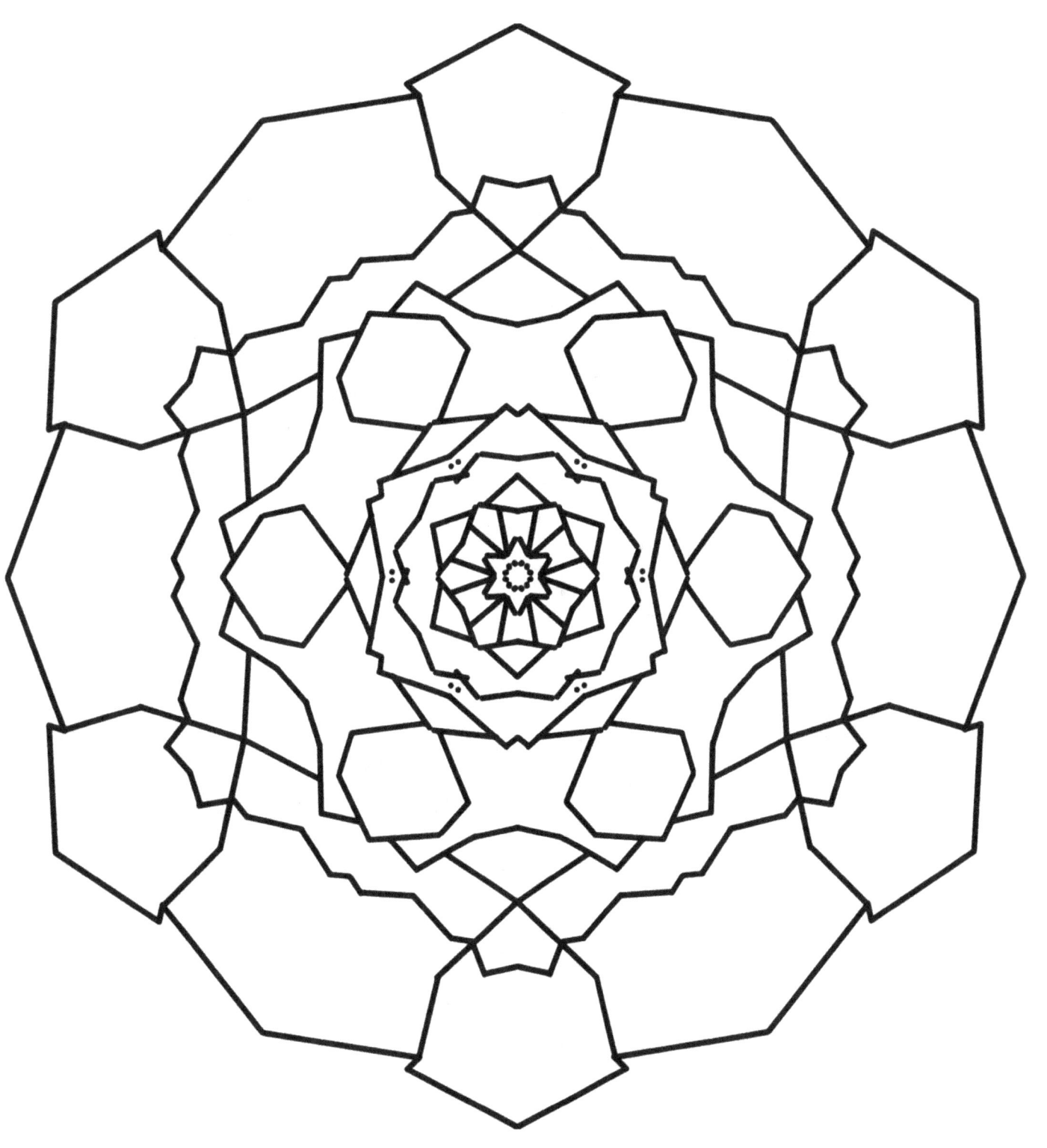

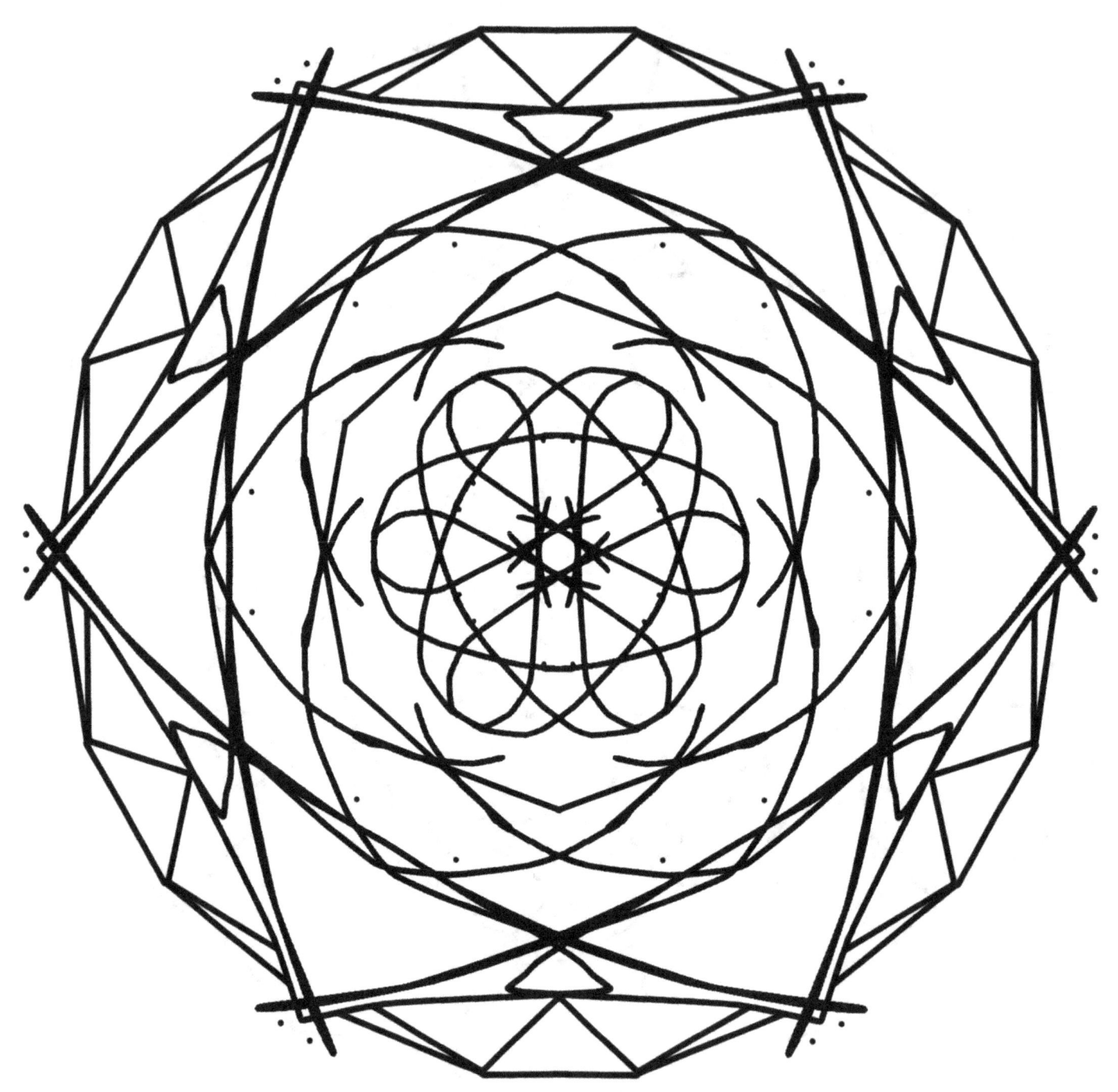

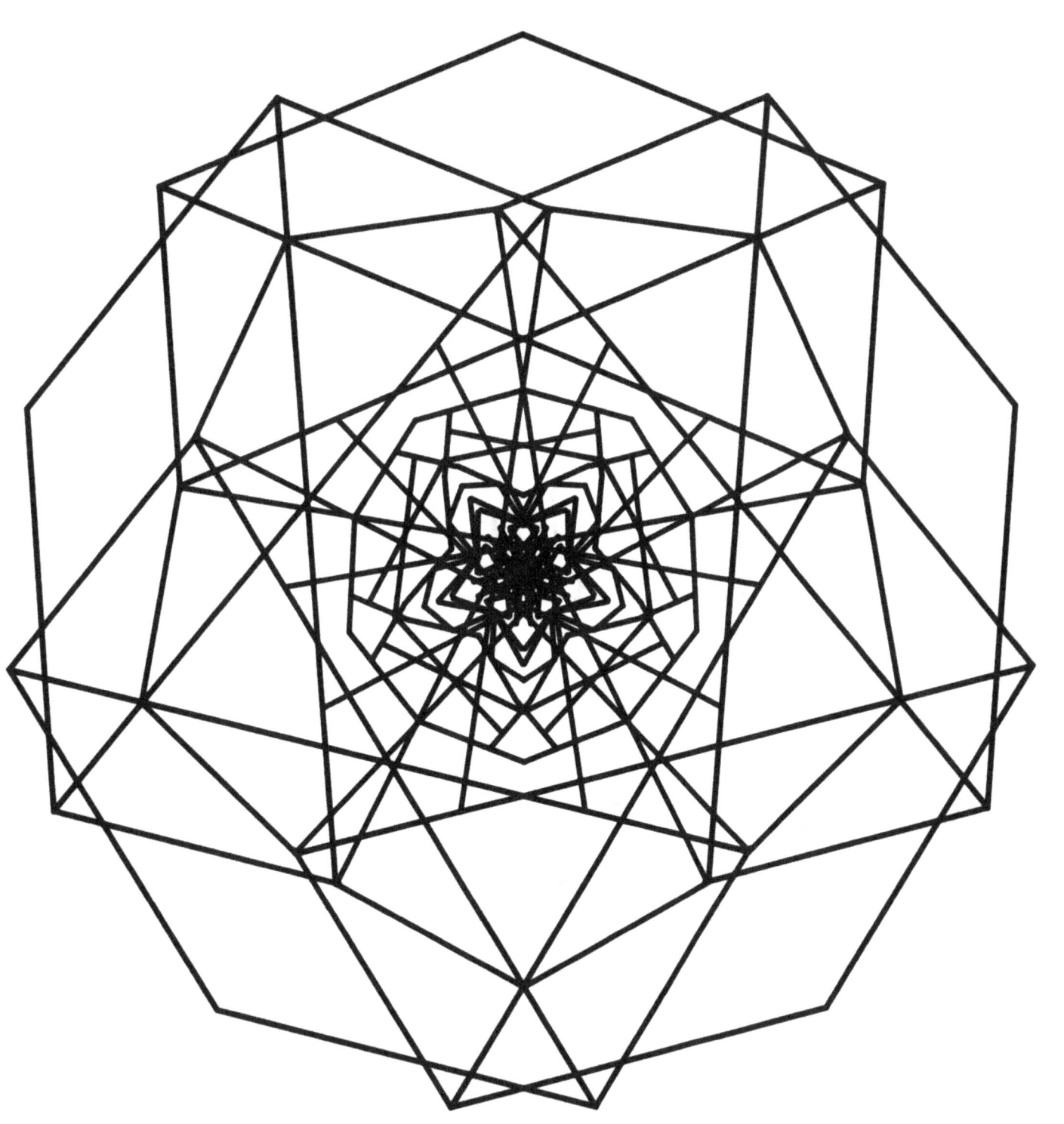

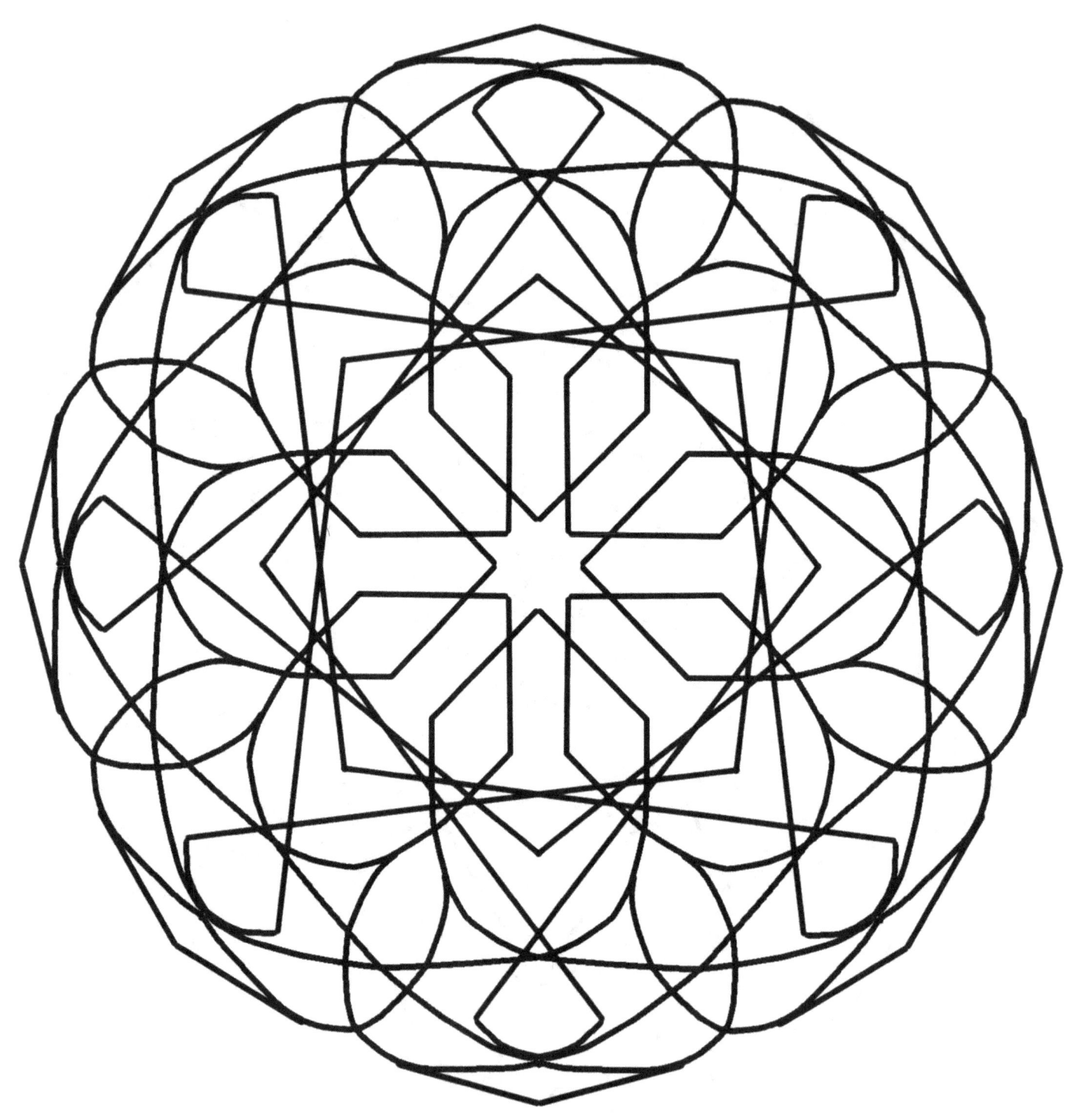

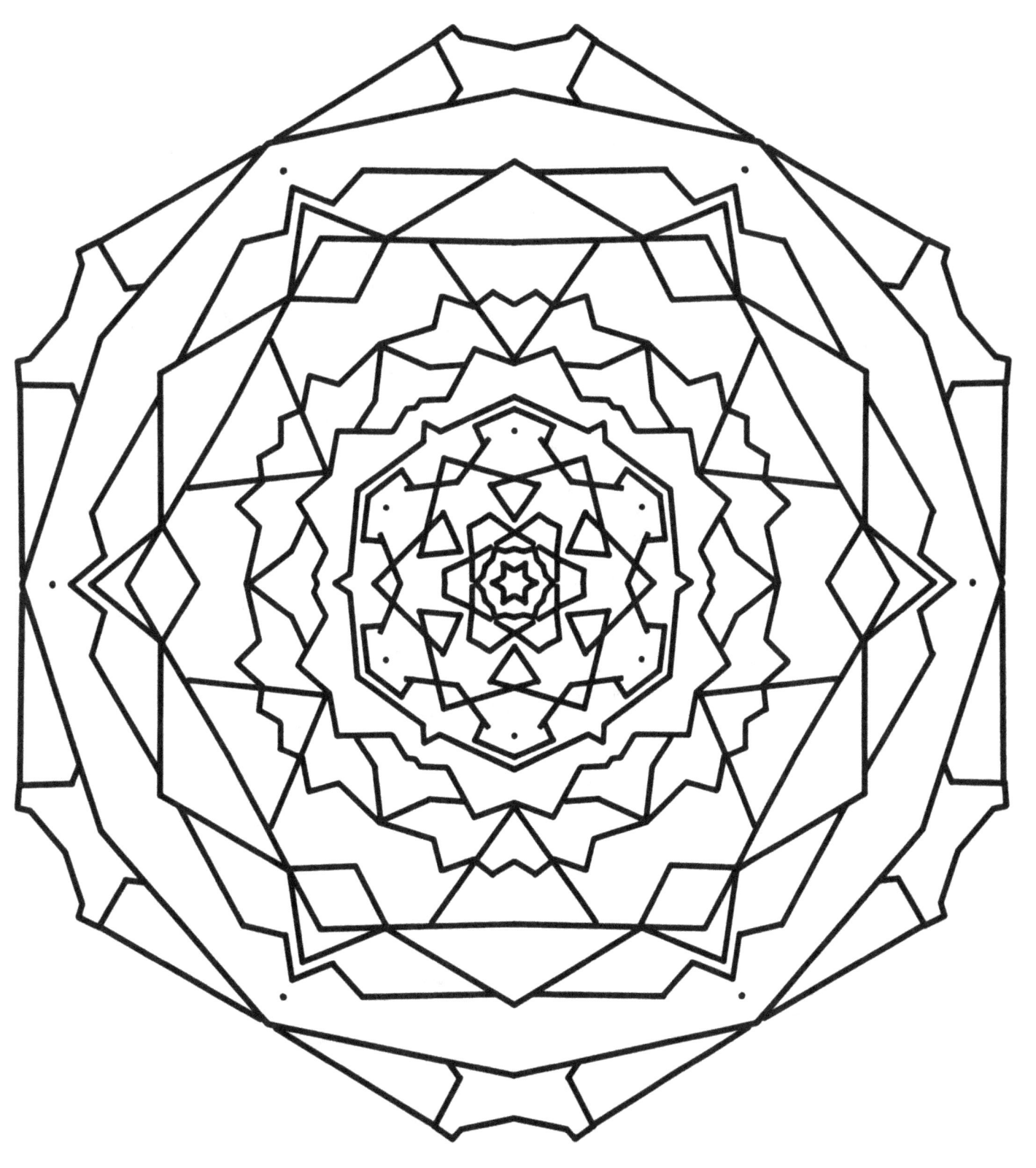

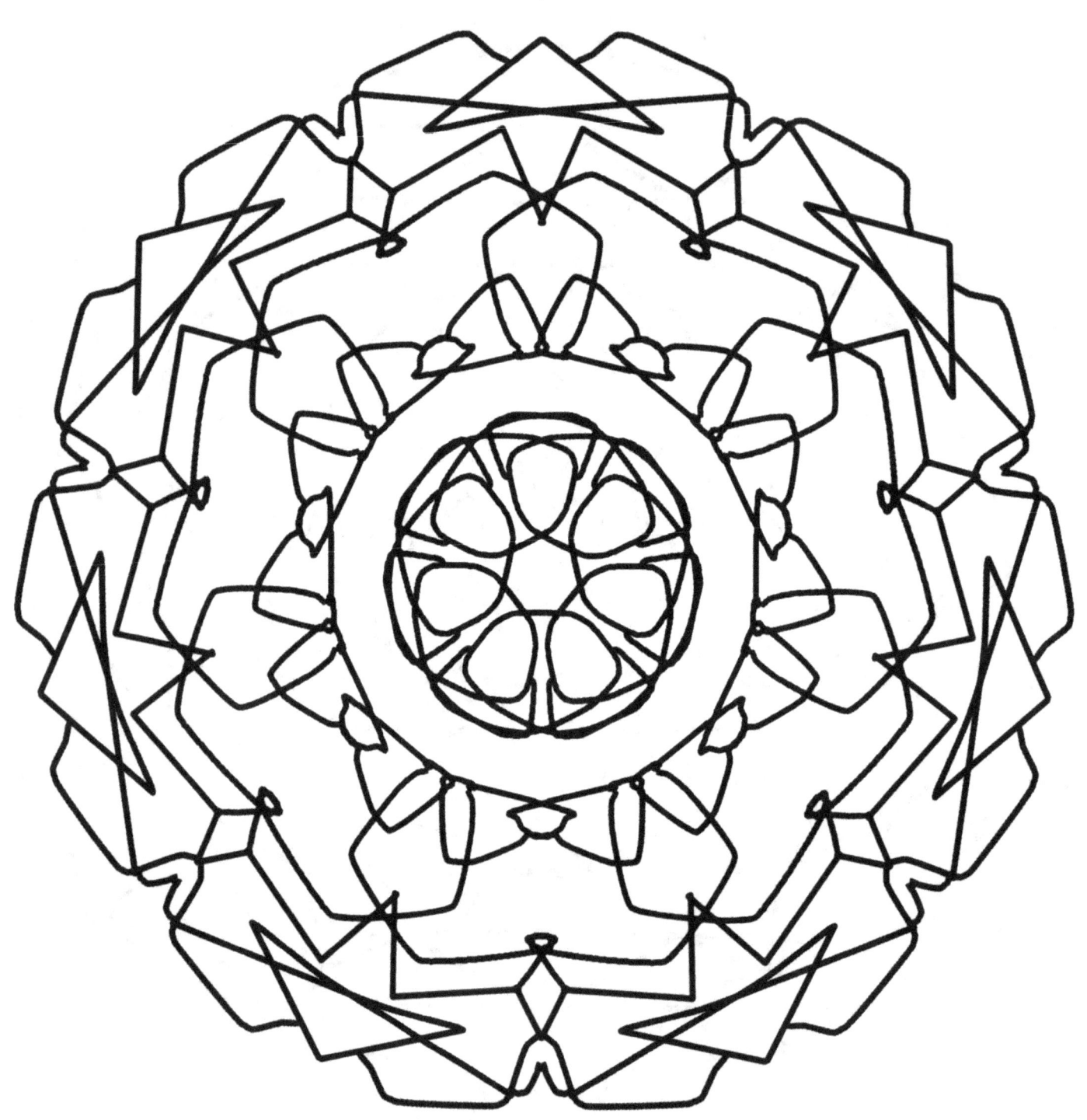

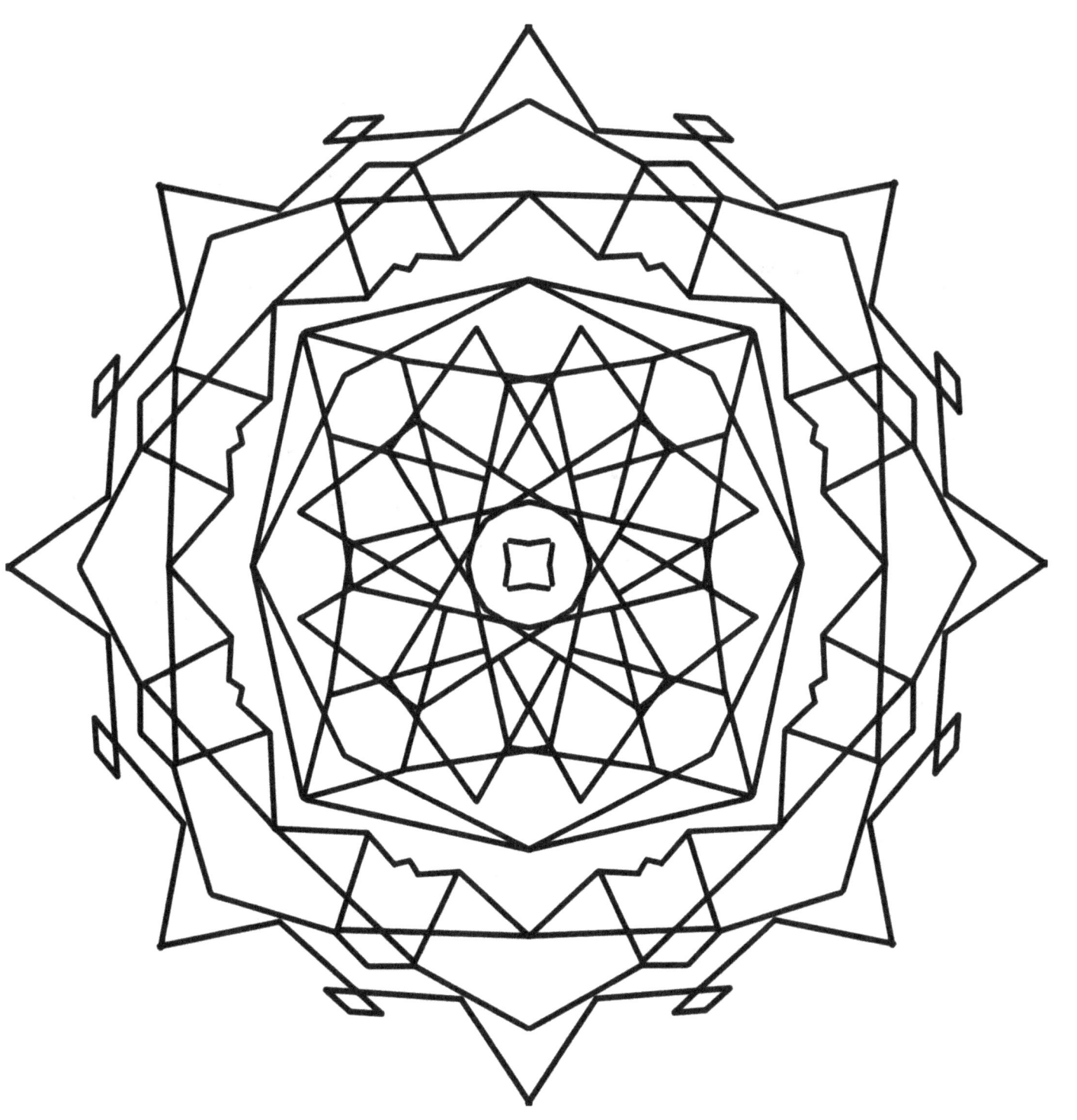

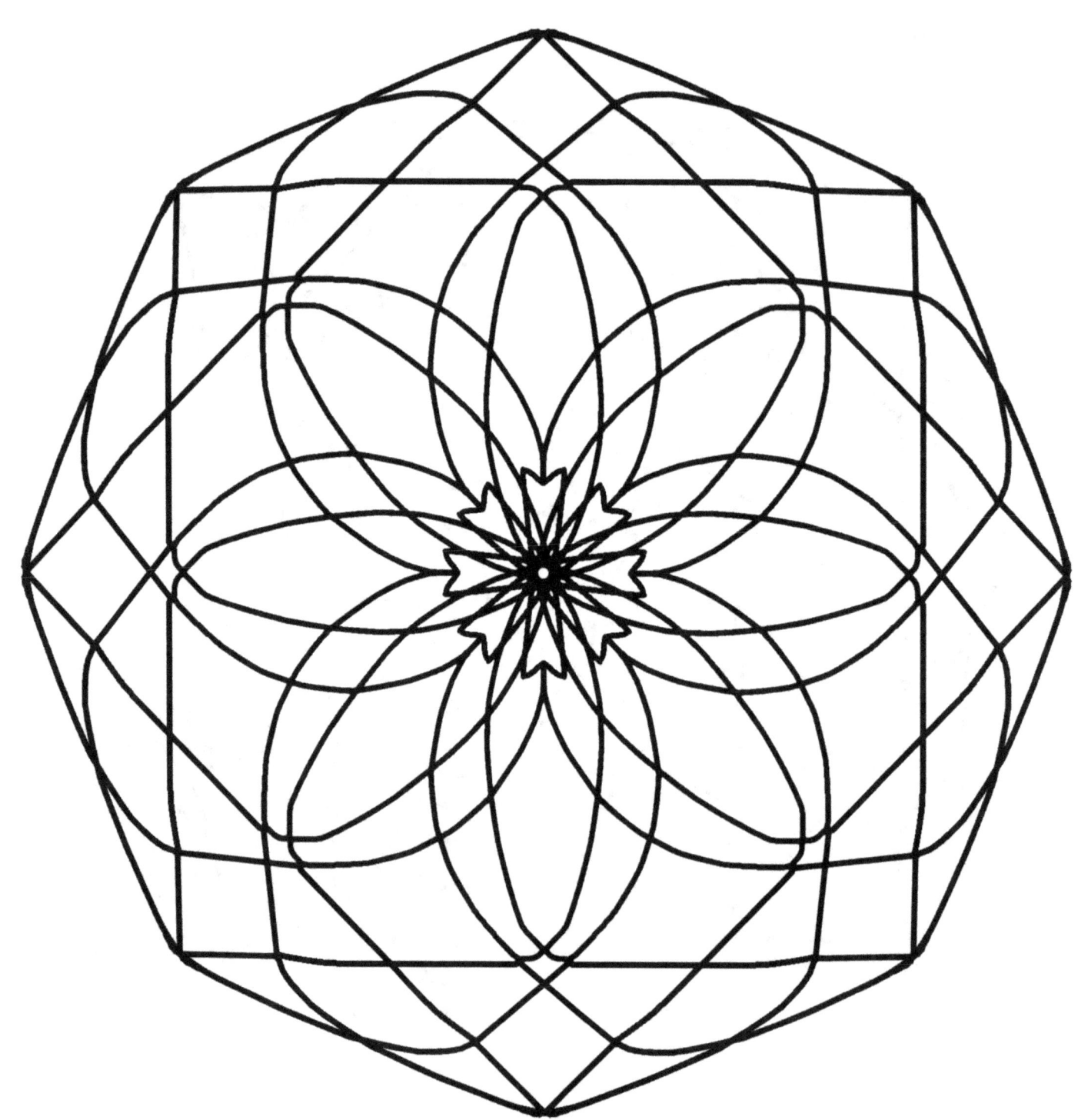

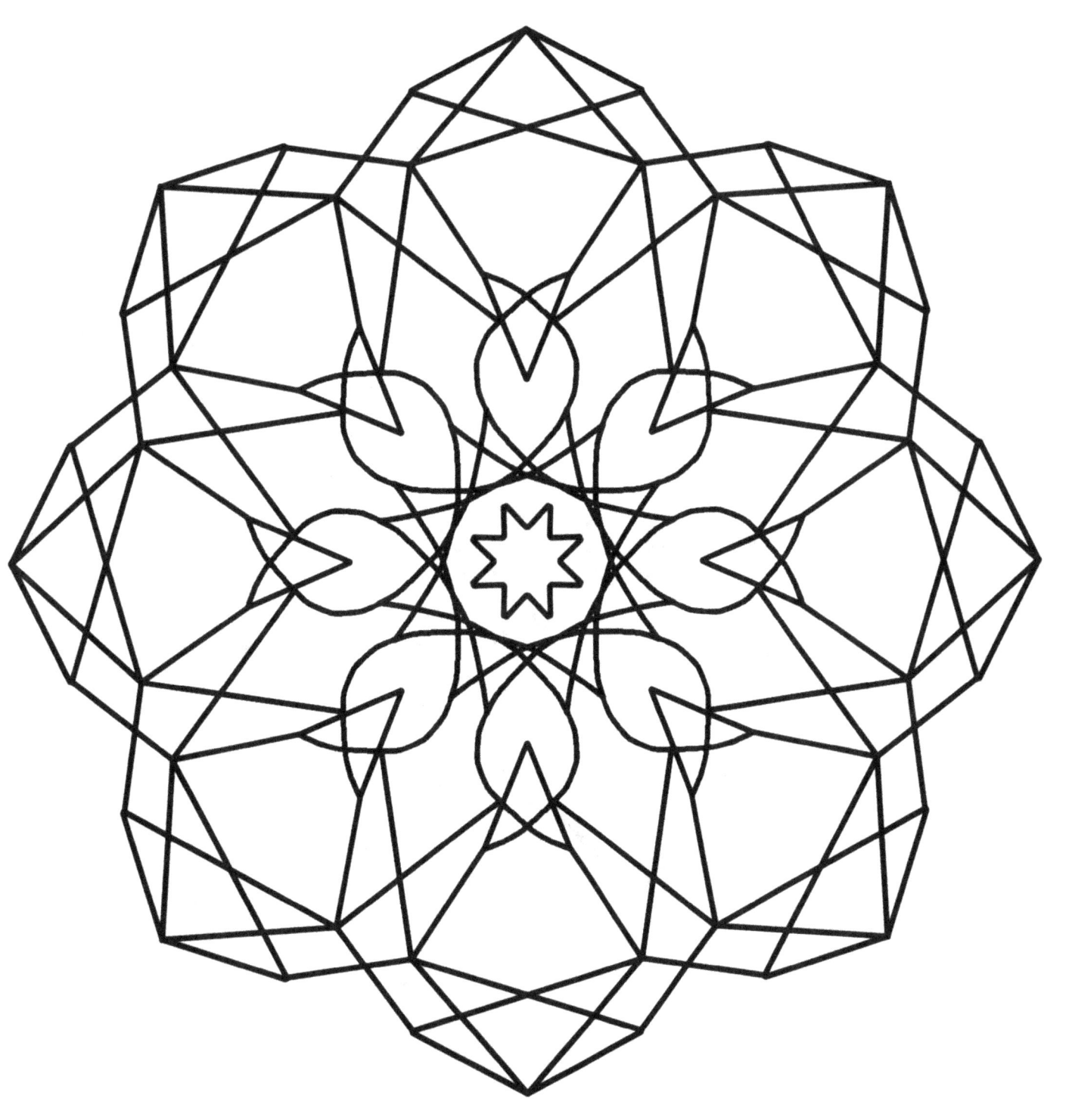

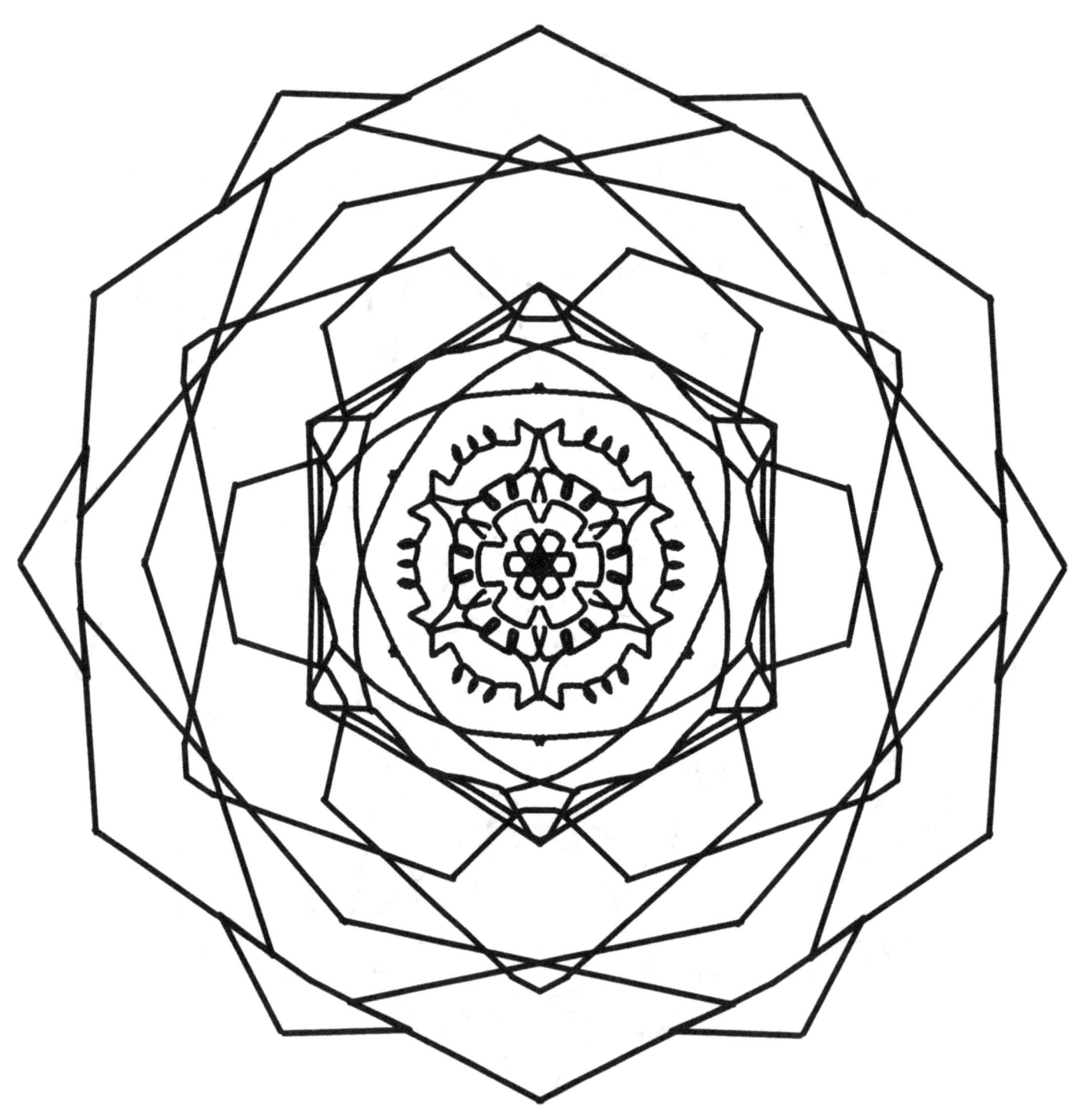

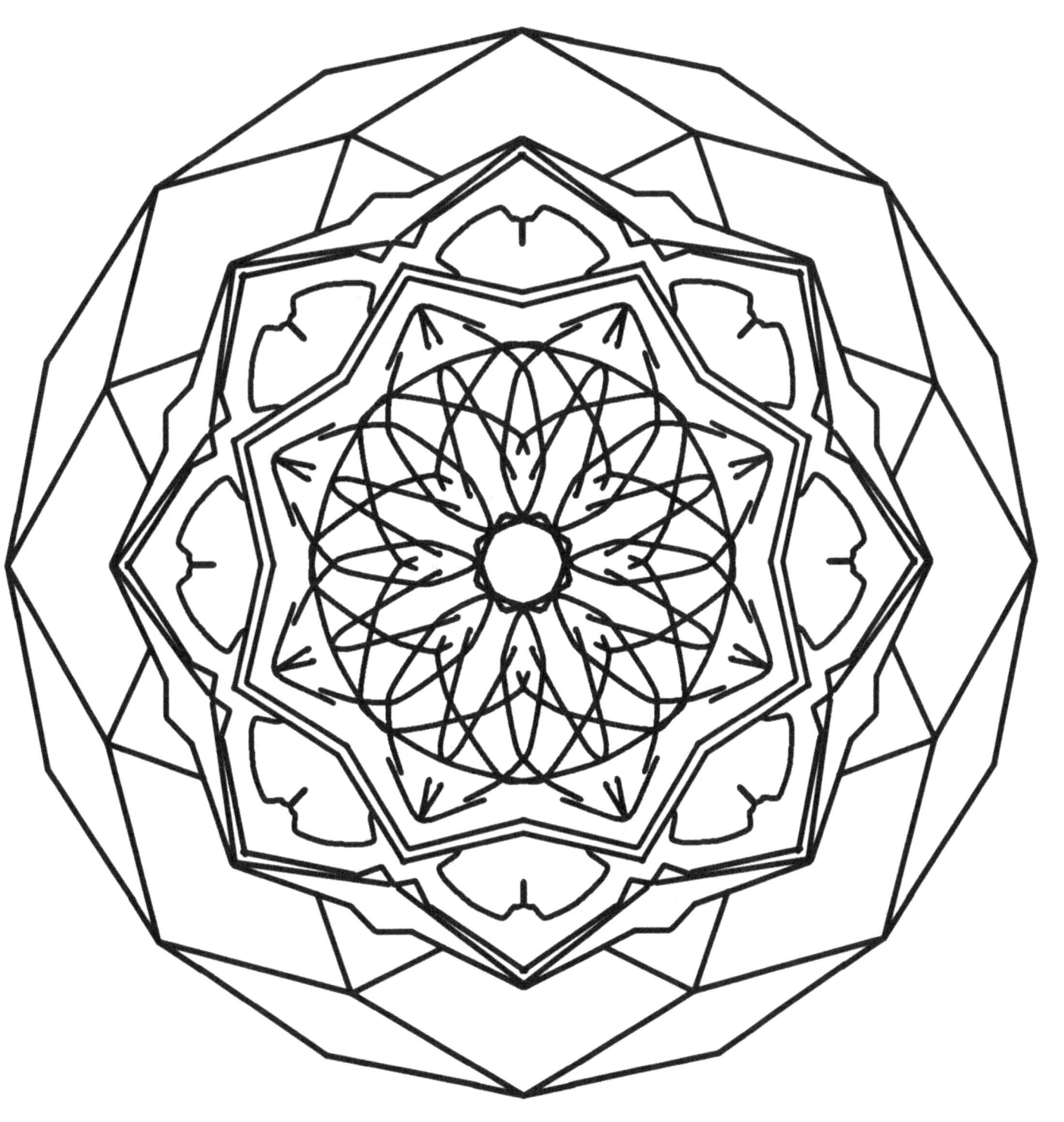

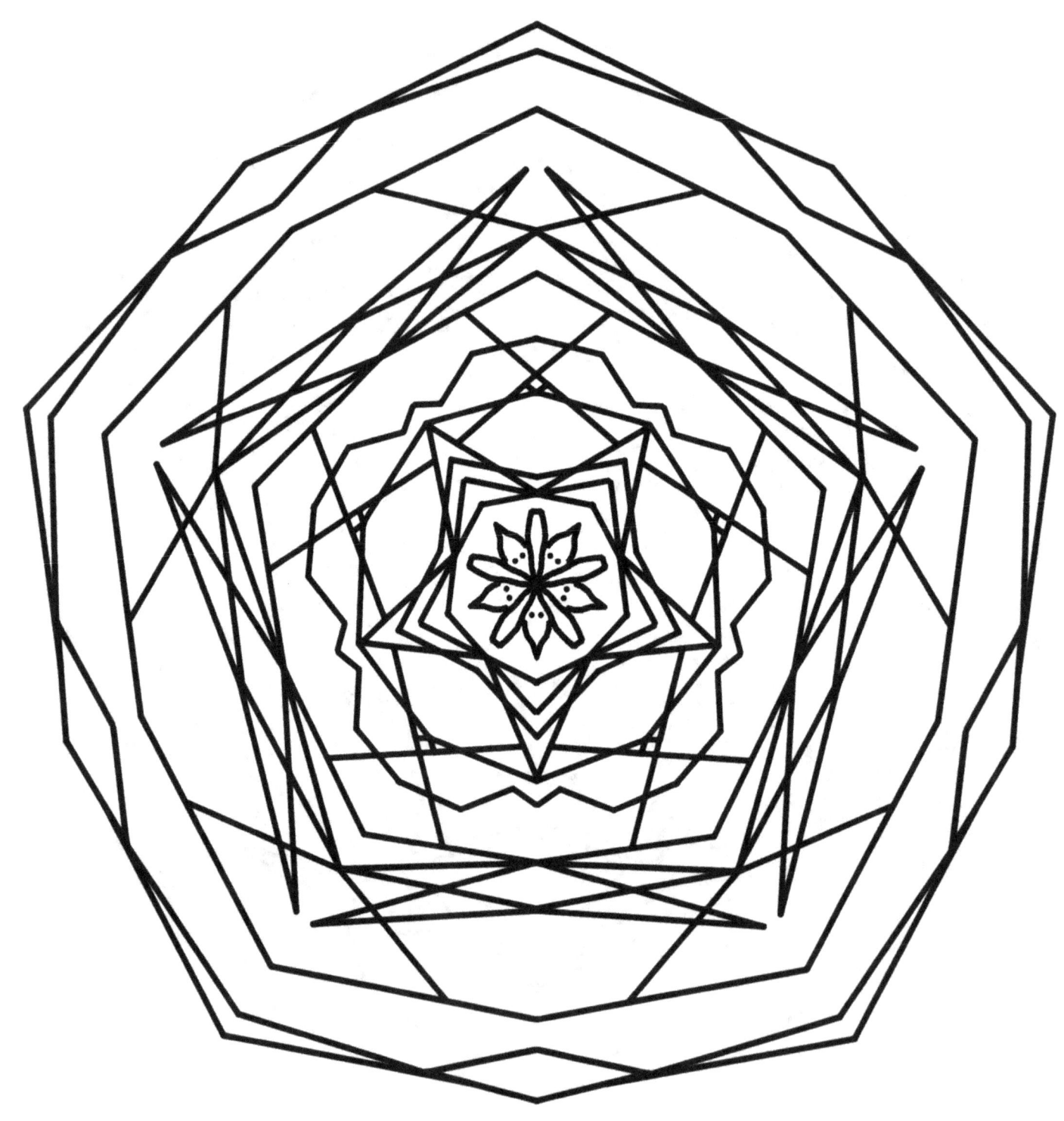

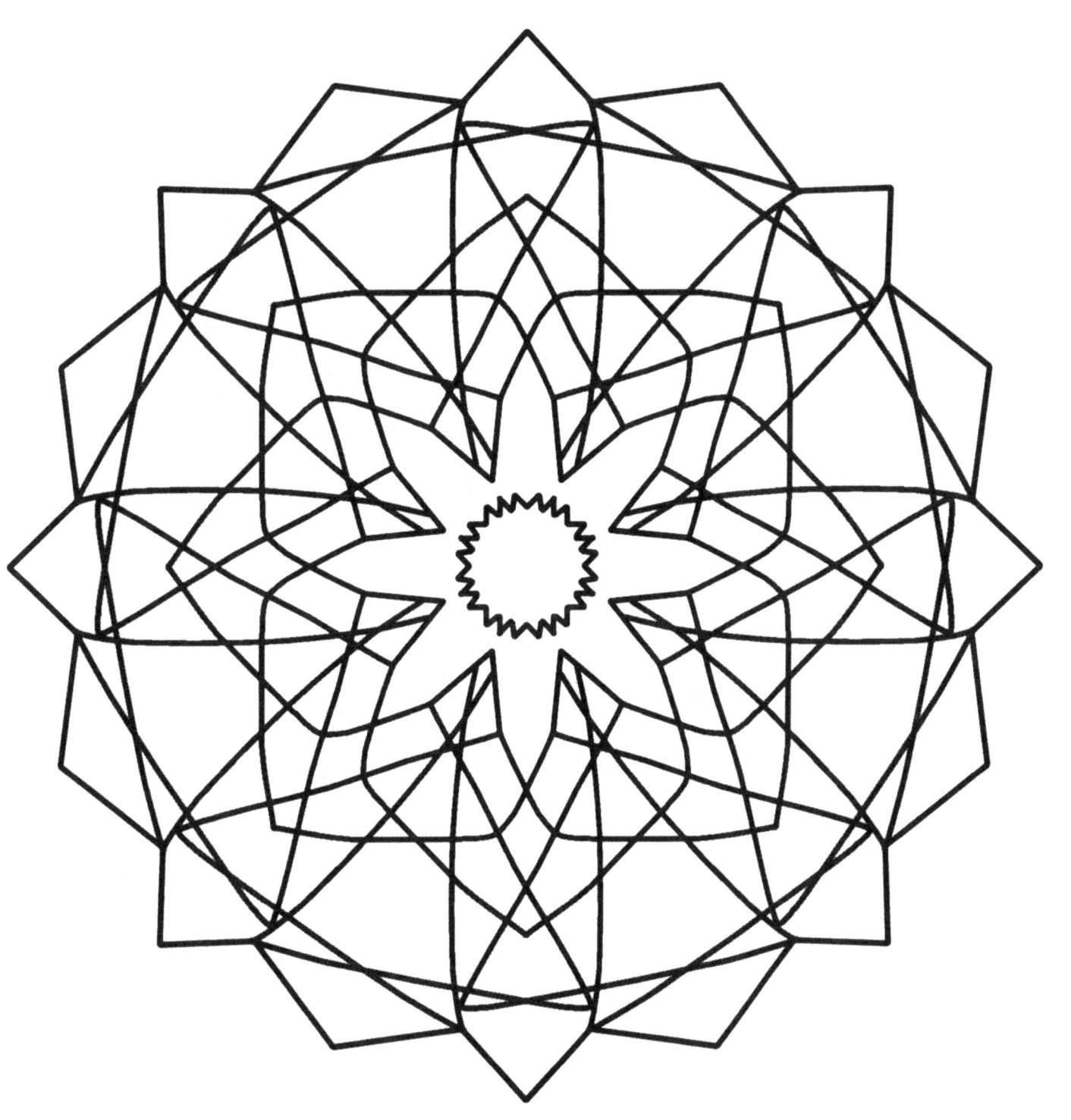

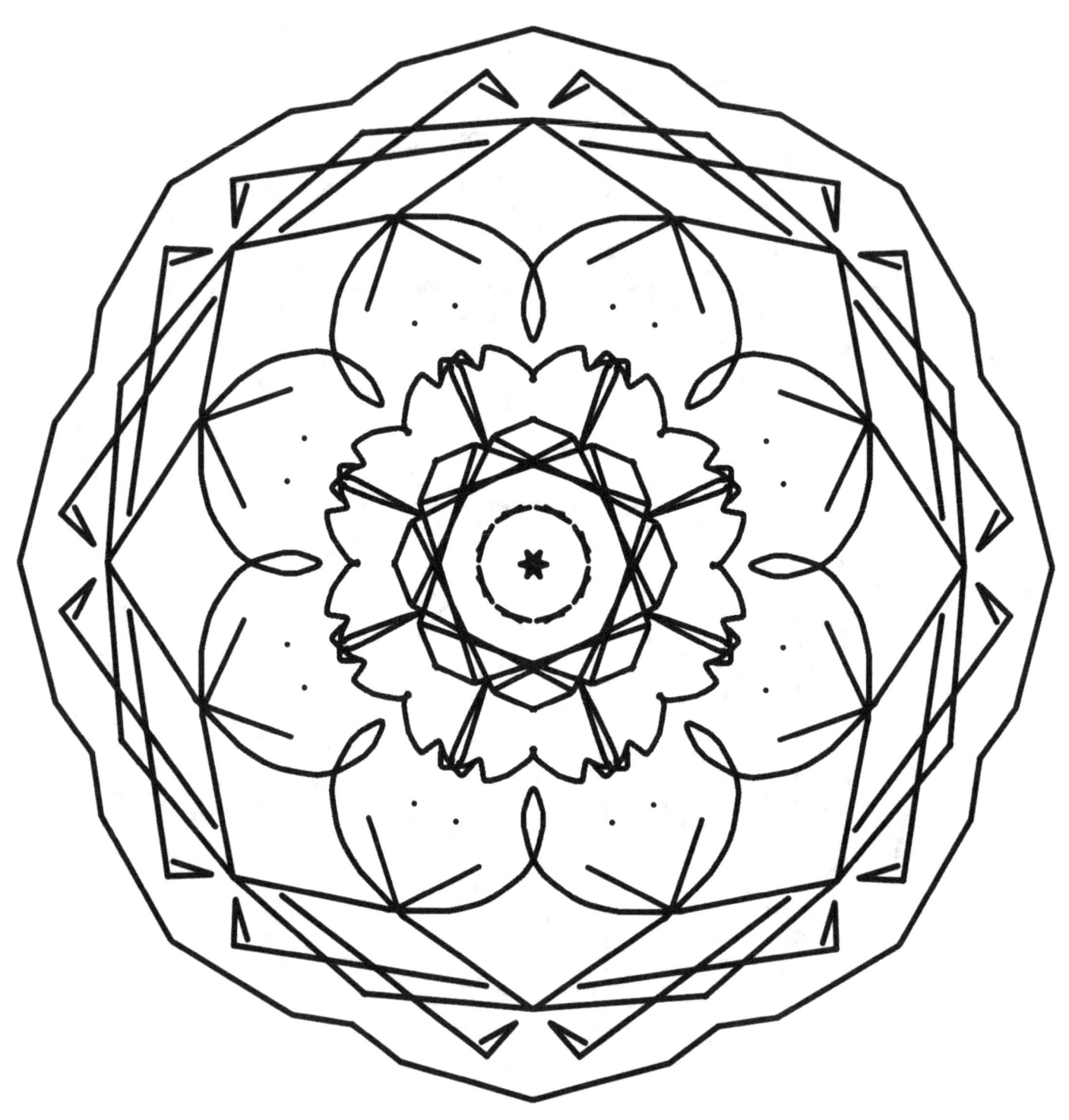

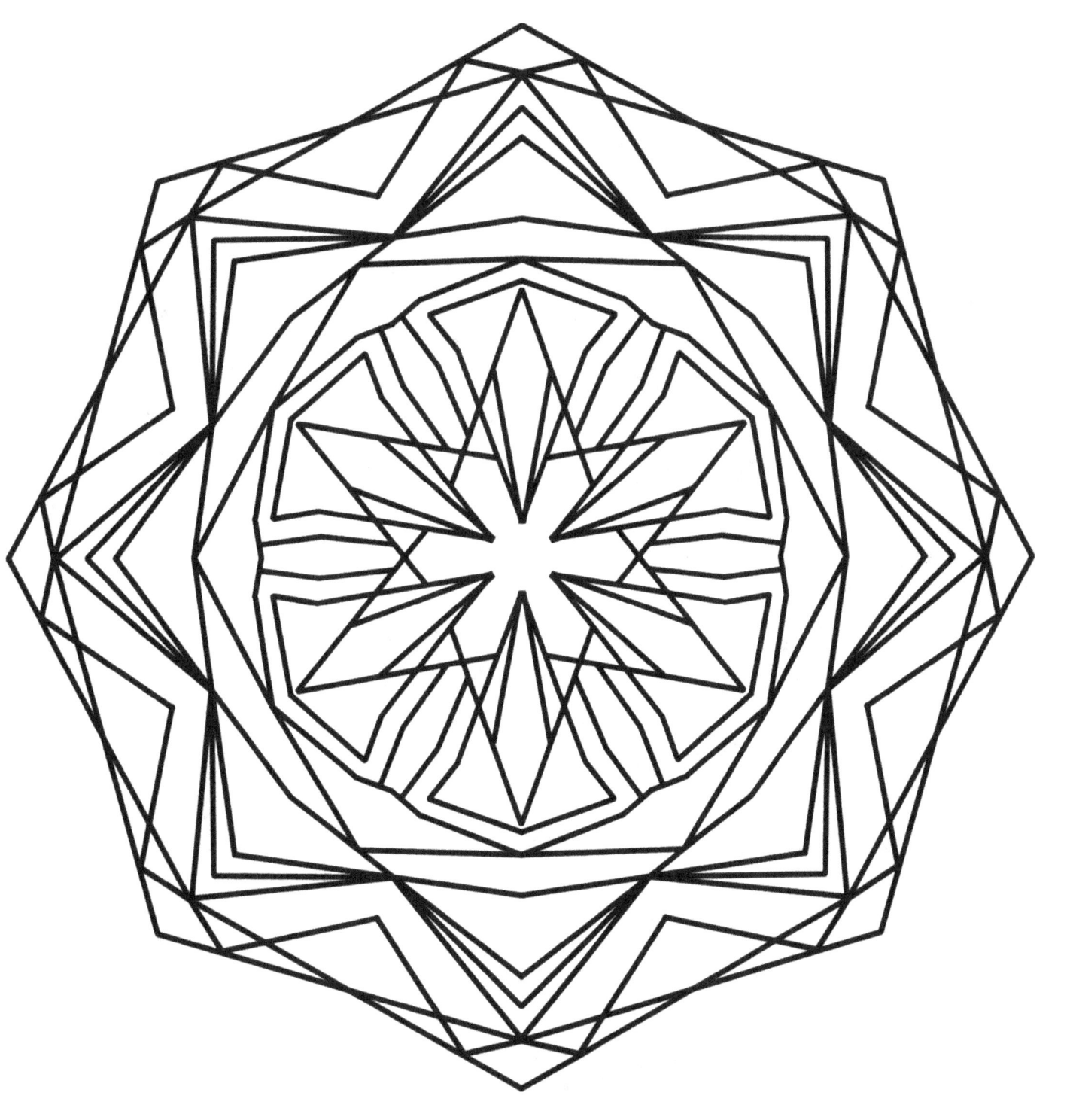

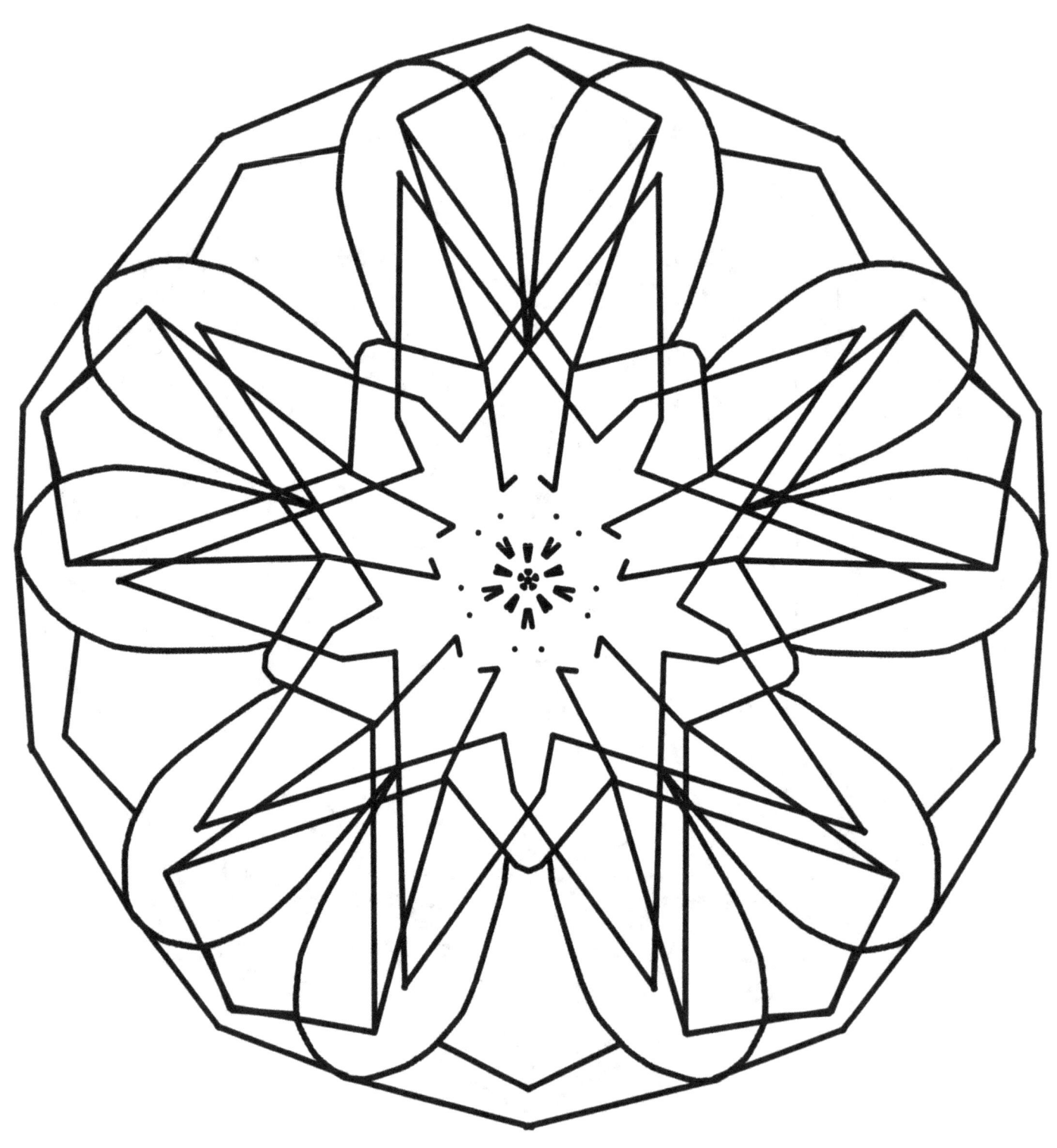

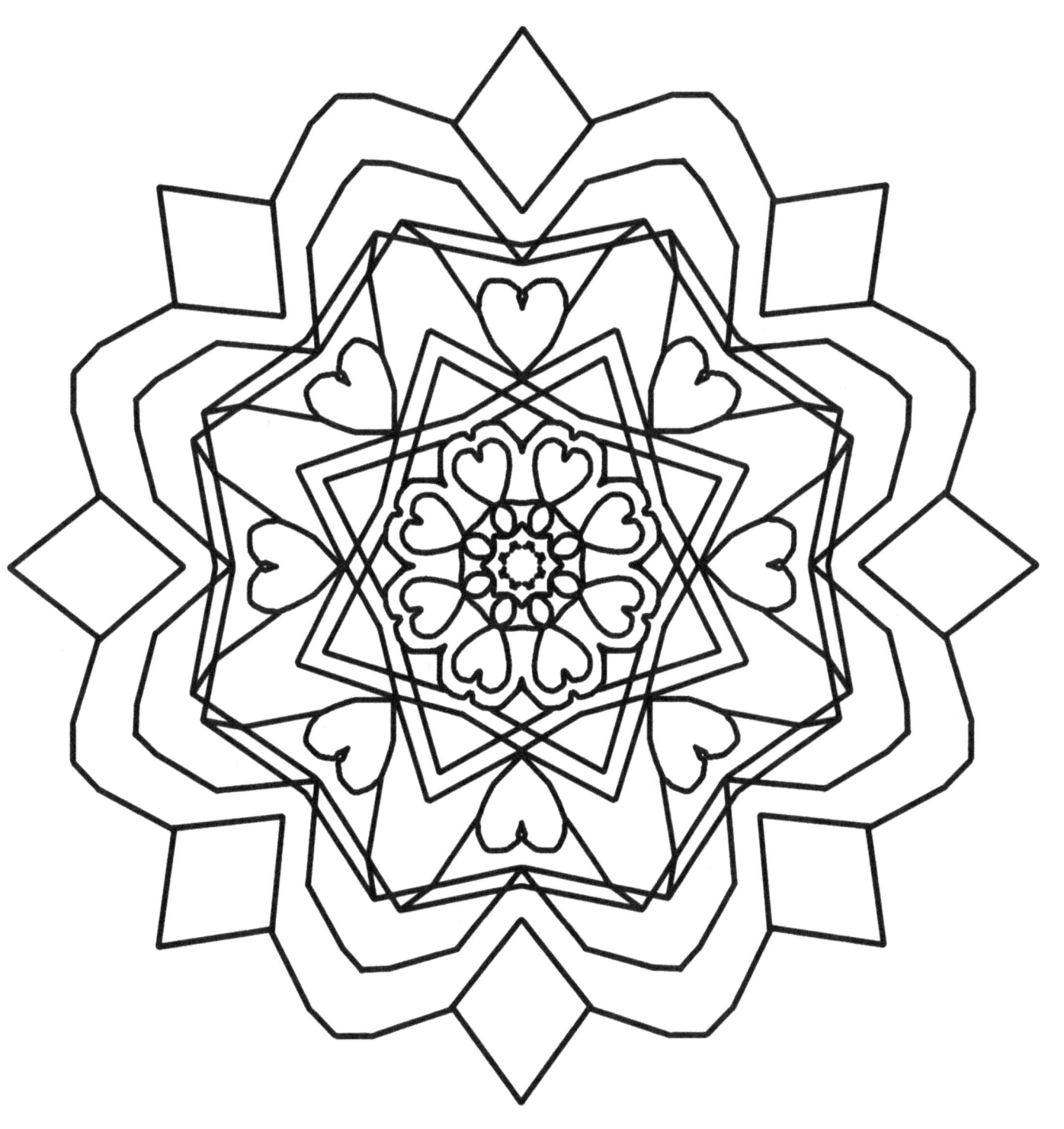

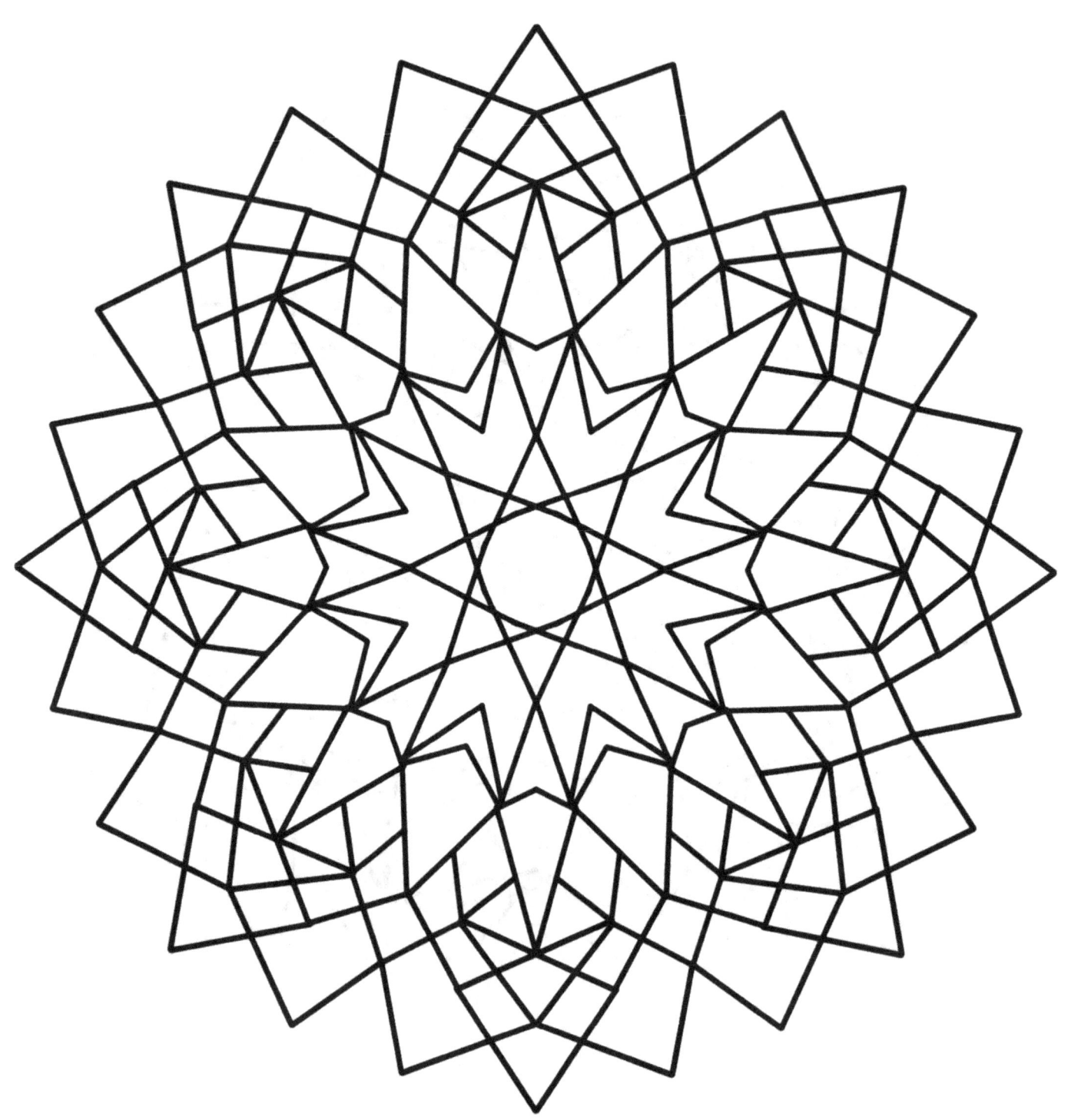

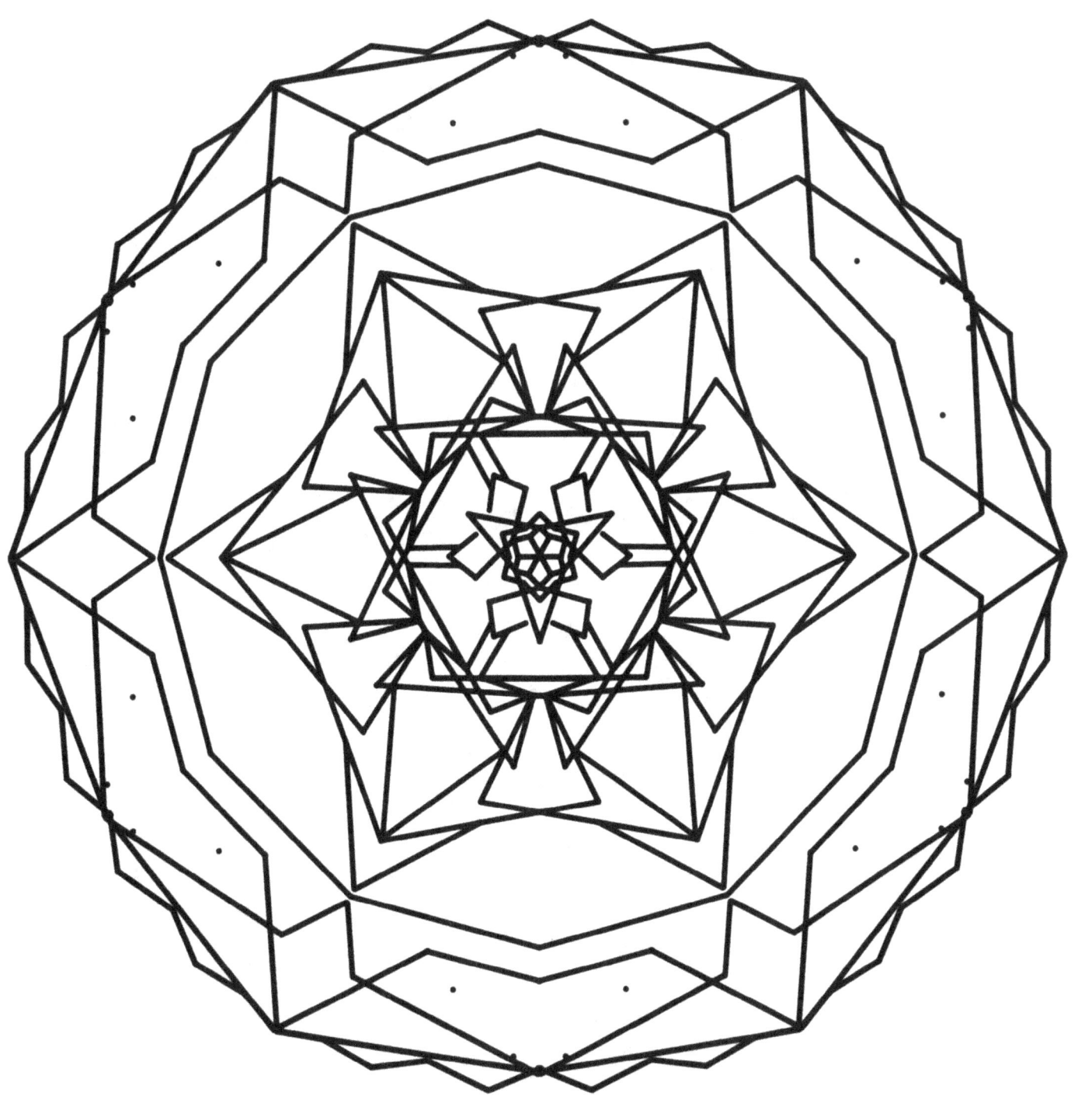

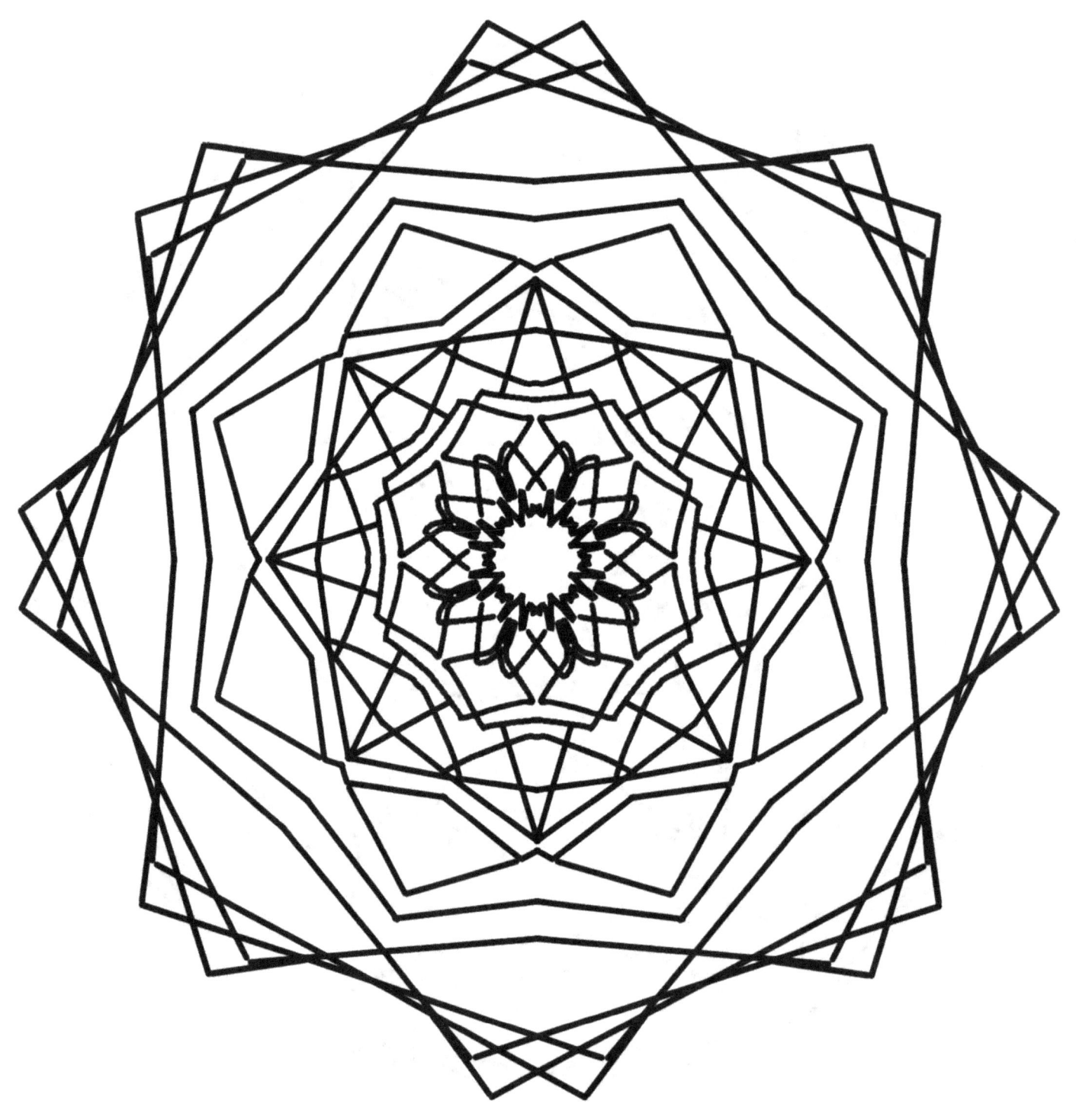

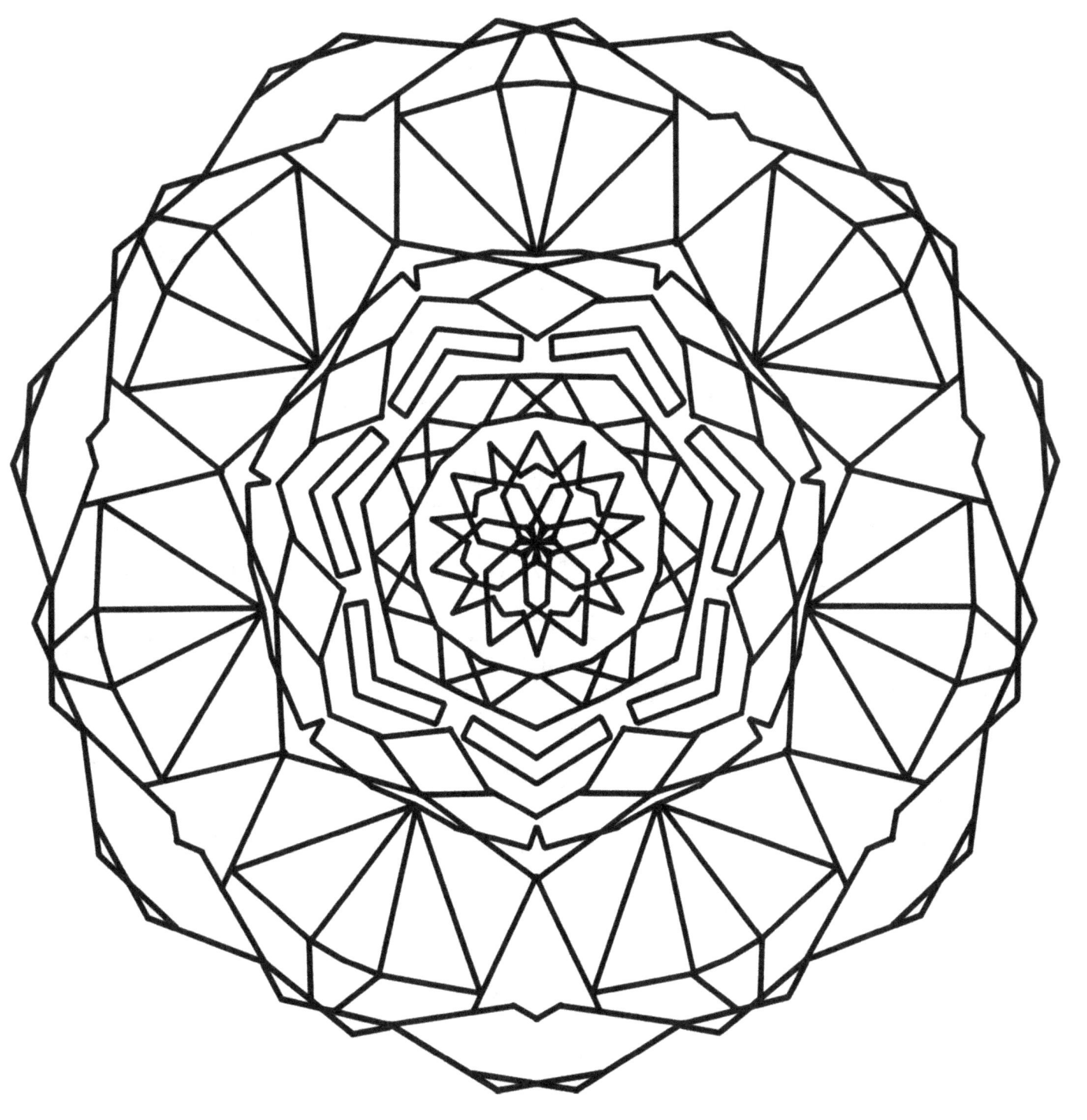

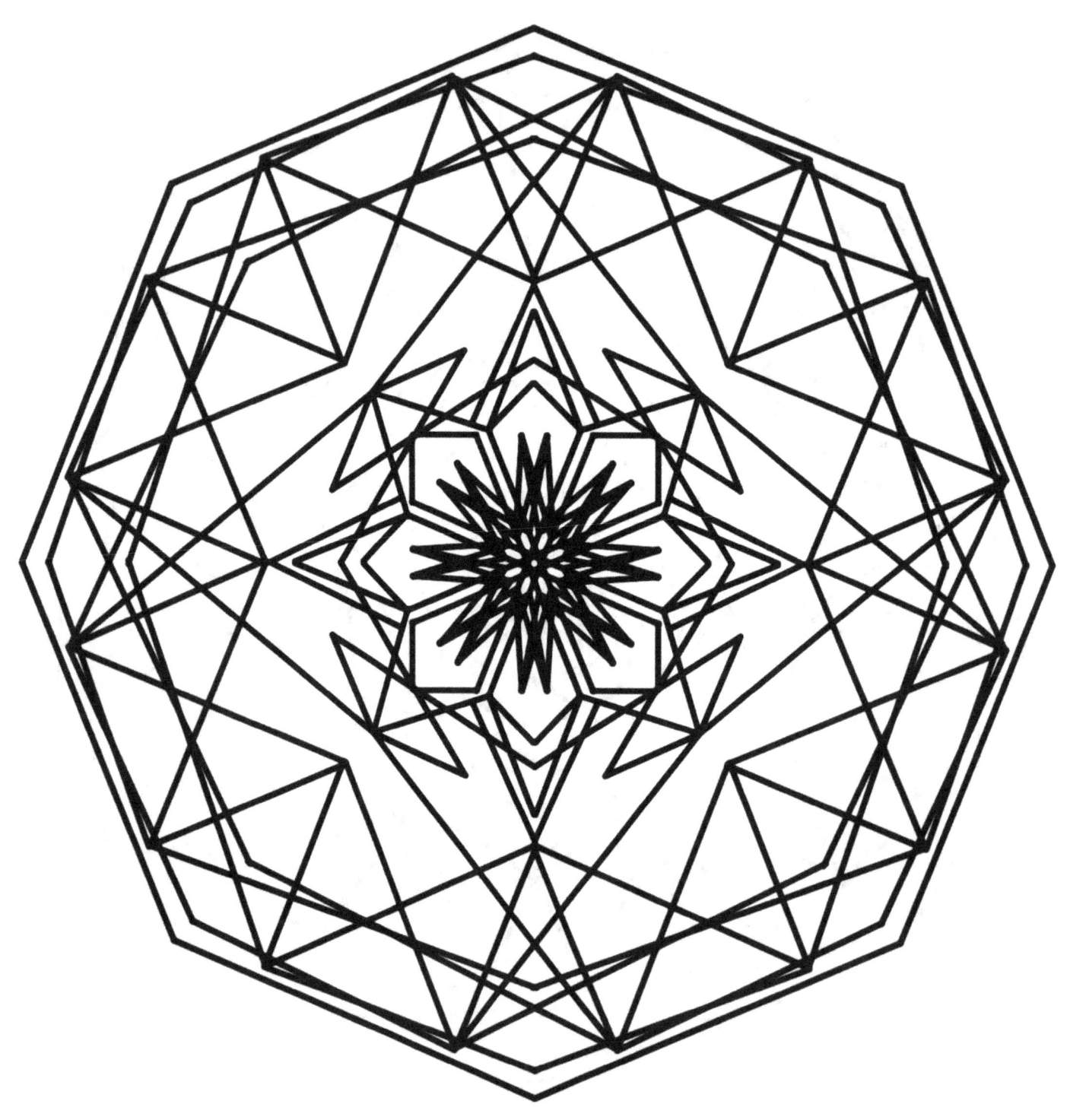

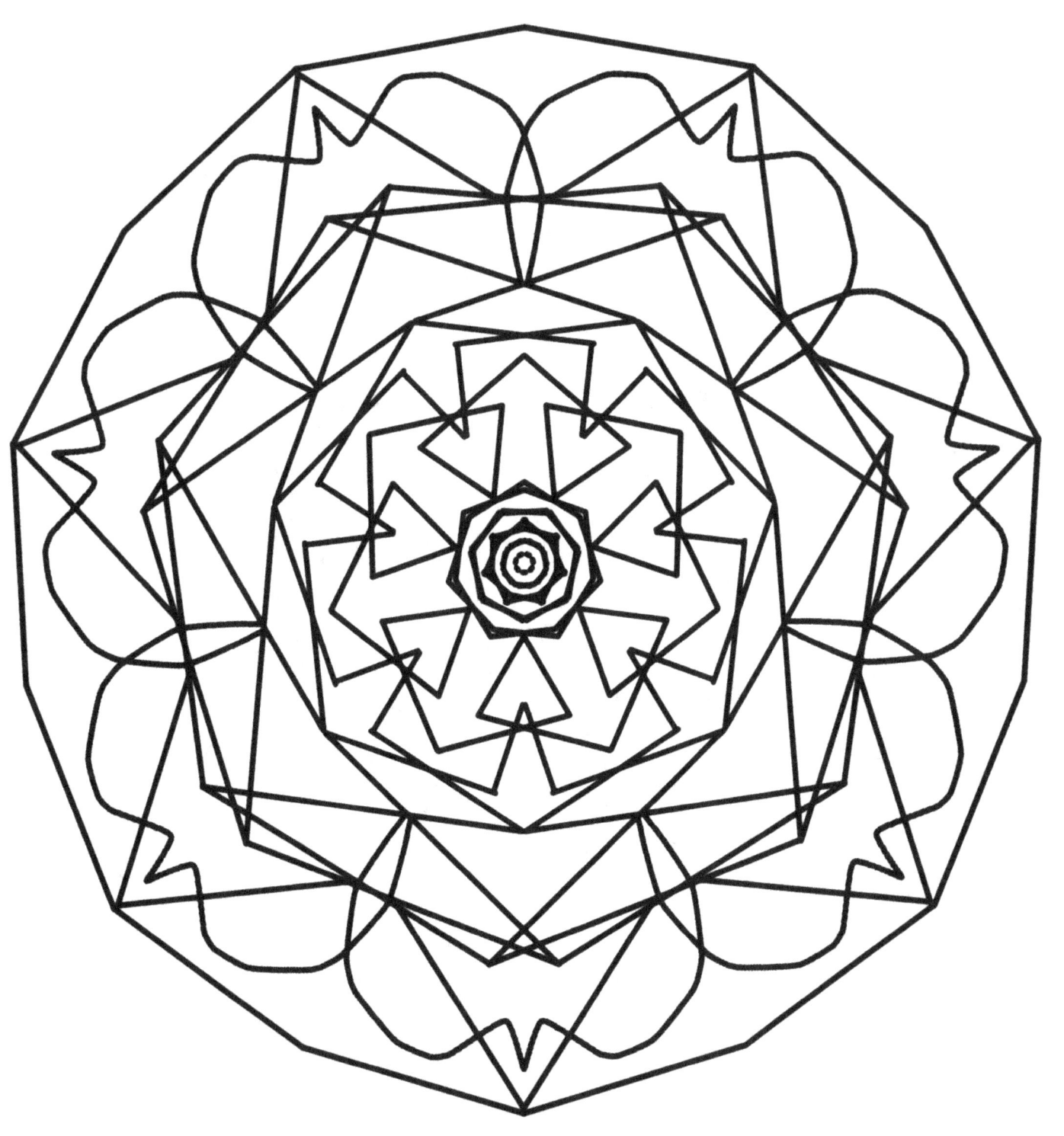

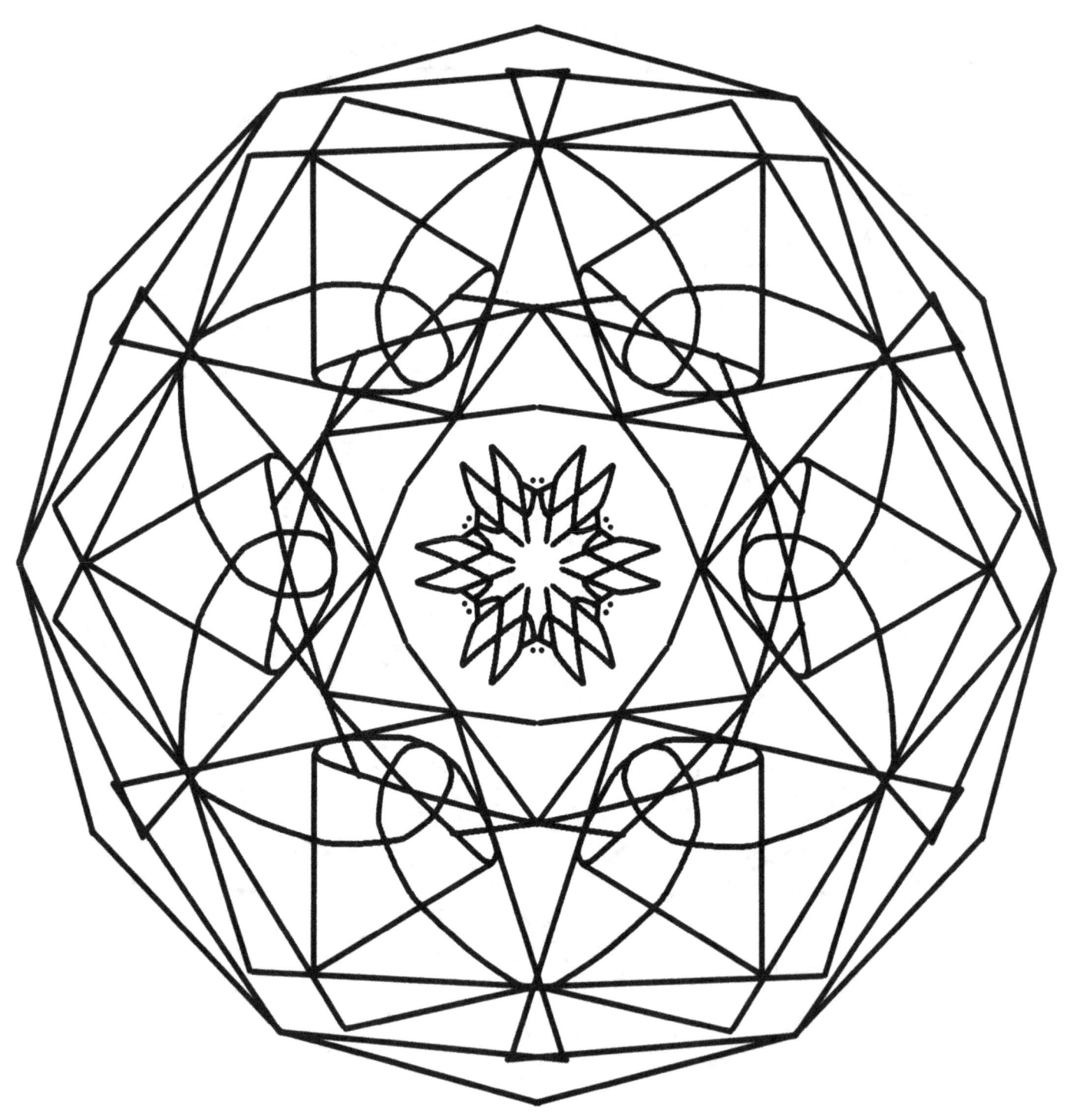

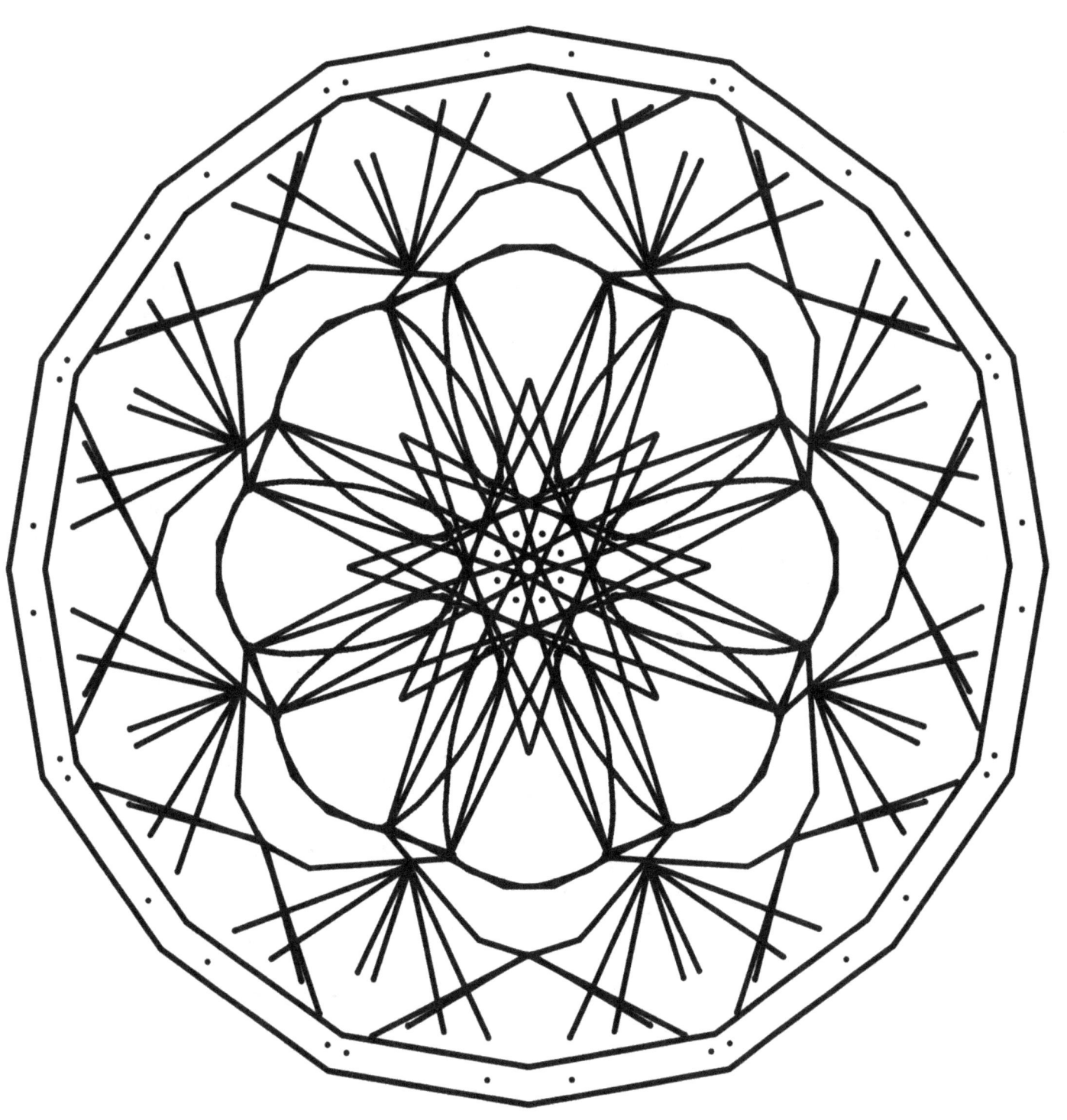

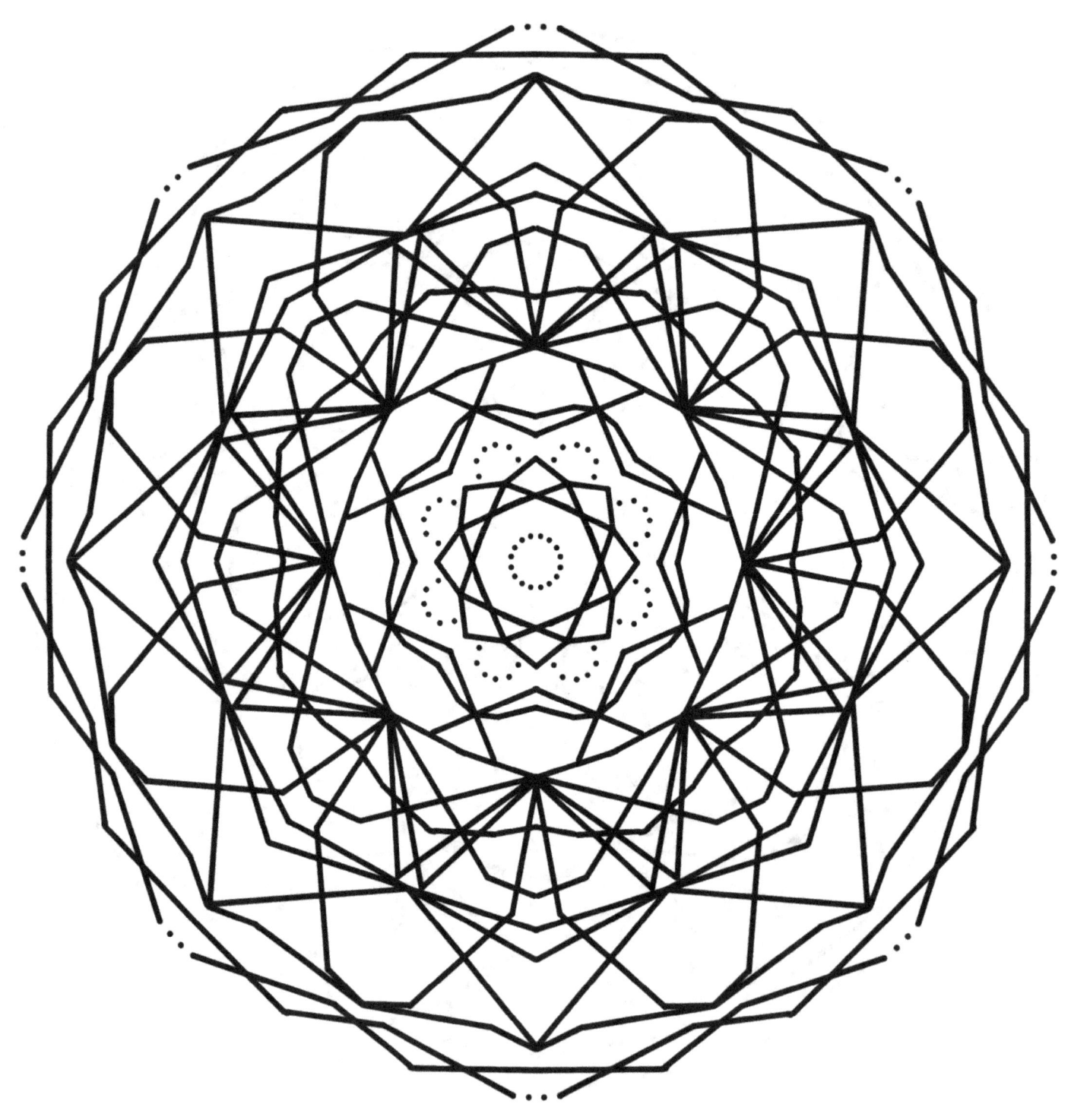

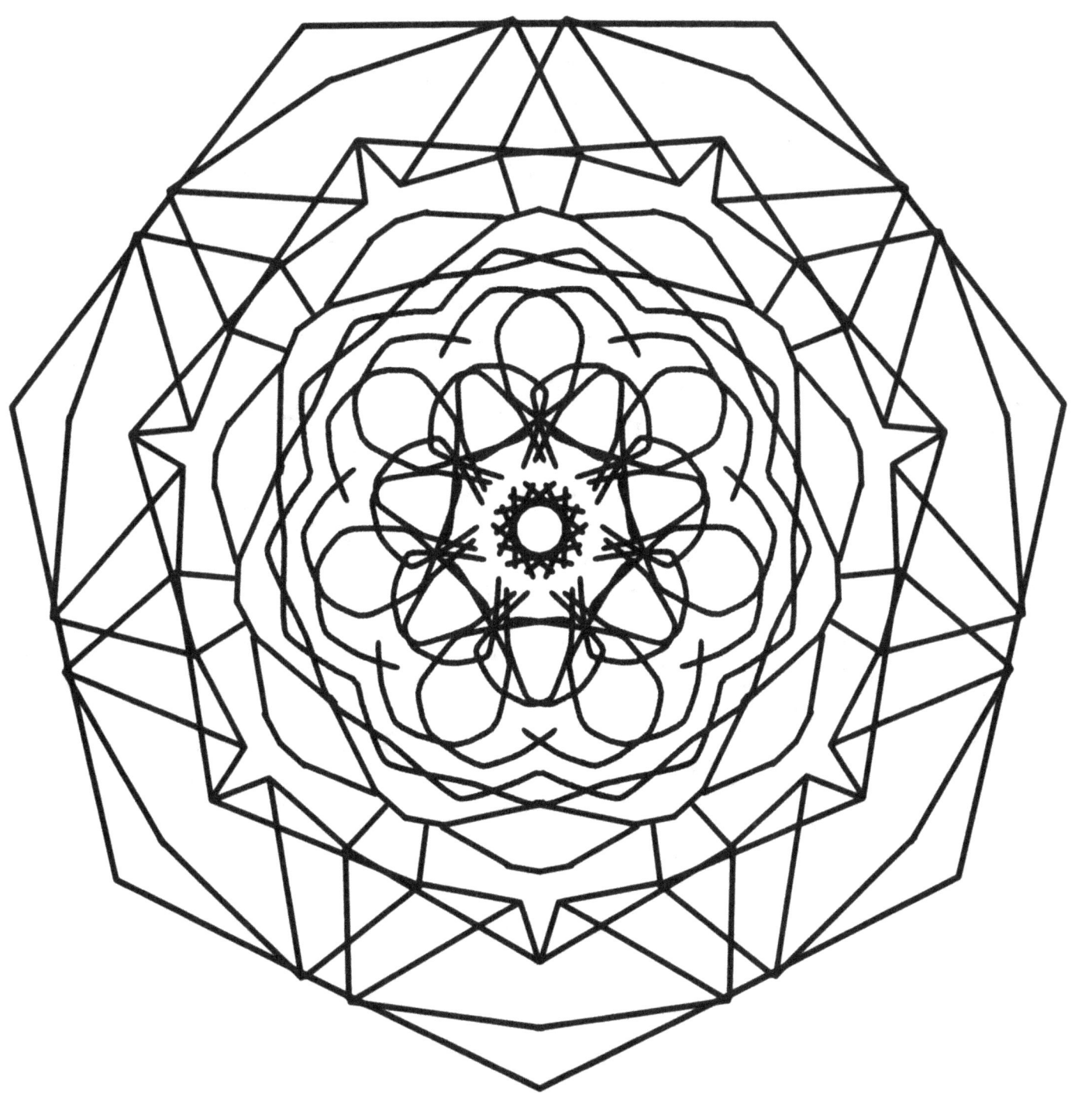

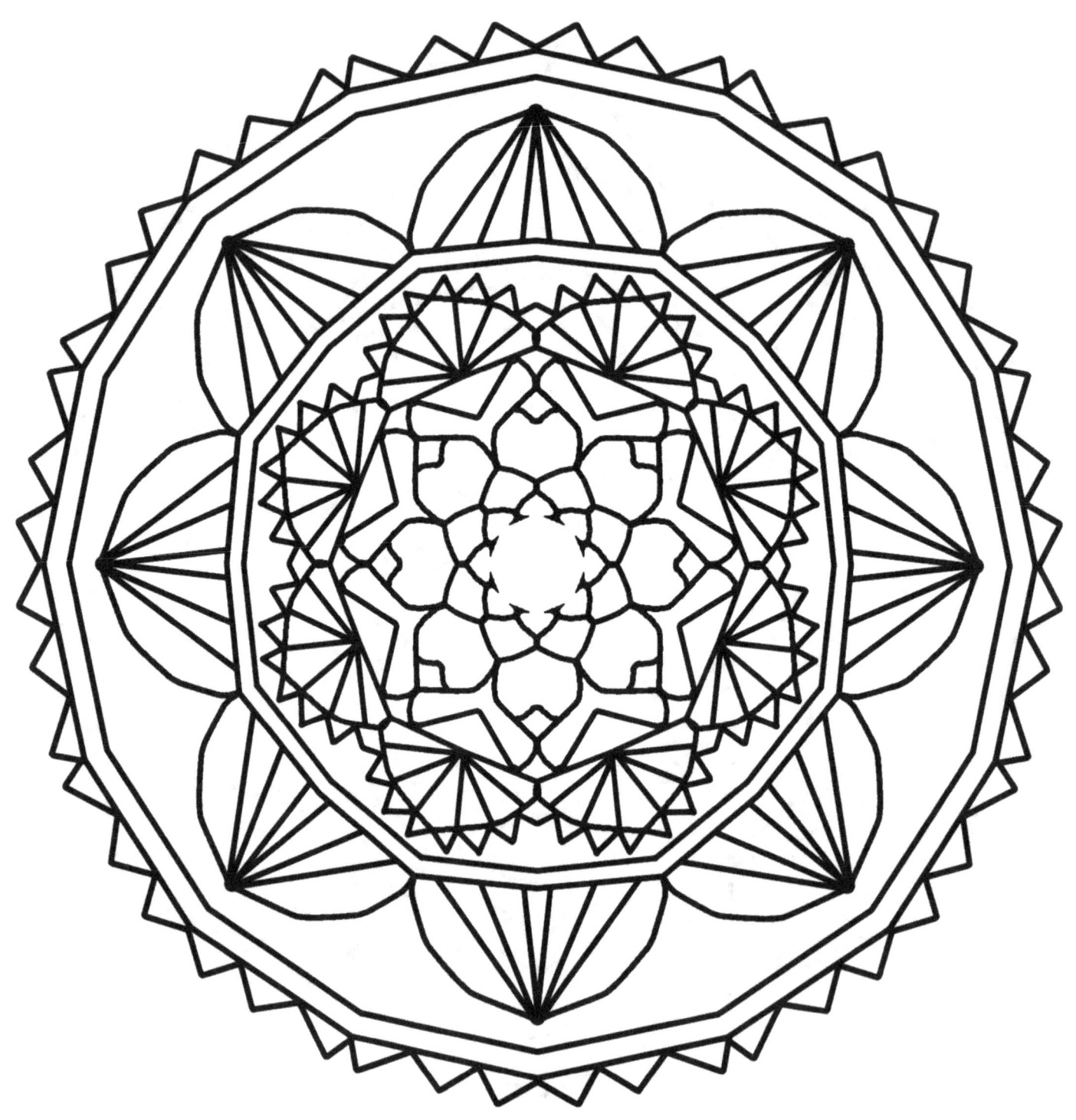

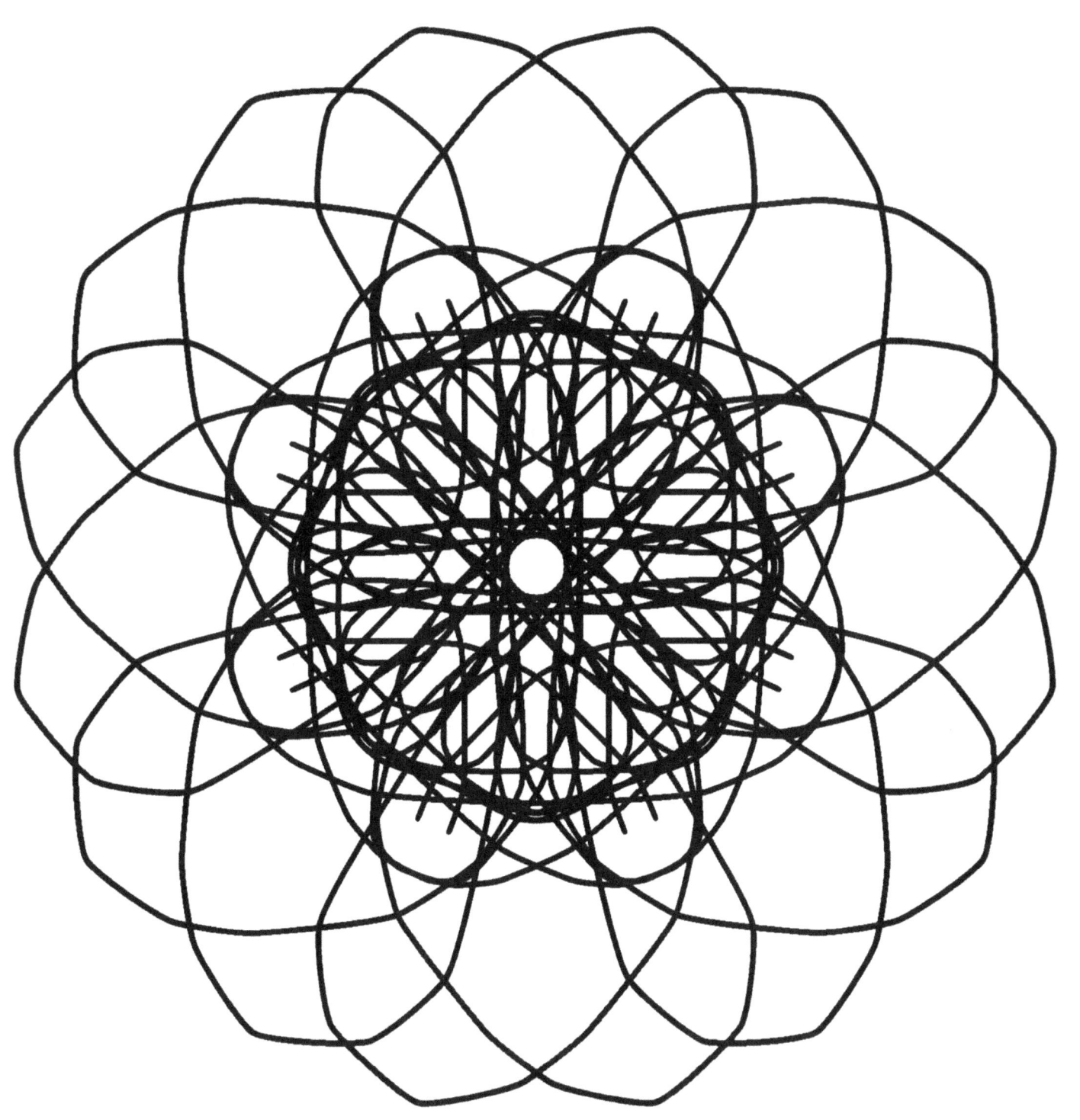

www.ingramcontent.com/pod-product-compliance
Lightning Source LLC
Chambersburg PA
CBHW060439220526
45465CB00008B/3195